RECORDS OF T

BEING

ENGLISH TRANSLATIONS

OF THE

ASSYRIAN AND EGYPTIAN MONUMENTS.

PUBLISHED UNDER THE SANCTION

OF

THE SOCIETY OF BIBLICAL ARCHÆOLOGY.

VOL. I.

LONDON:

SAMUEL BAGSTER AND SONS,

15, PATERNOSTER ROW.

RECORDS OF THE PAST:

BEING

ENGLISH TRANSLATIONS

OF THE

ASSYRIAN AND EGYPTIAN MONUMENTS.

VOL. I.

ASSYRIAN TEXTS.

NOTE.

Every Text here given is either now translated for the *first time*, or has been specially revised by the Author to the date of this publication.

PREFACE.

THE present volume of translations of Babylonian and Assyrian inscriptions, in the cuneiform or arrowheaded character, is the first of a series intended to place before the public the important results of the study and interpretation of these and Egyptian monuments, by English and foreign students. The value of these translations, to those interested in Biblical history and archæology, cannot be estimated too highly by all who have turned their attention to the language, literature, and history of the nations of the East contemporaneous with the Hebrews, and conterminous to the land of Palestine. As many of the texts are of the most remote antiquity, they derive from that fact alone the greatest importance, detailing contemporaneous events which had hitherto escaped notice, been lost, or else imperfectly transmitted by secondary sources. In order to render the volume as popular as possible, and make the information afforded as simple as it can be given, the translations are only accompanied by such notes as are absolutely required to explain intelligibly a few of the more obscure passages. The doubtful portions of the translations are printed in italics, and additional words are indicated by brackets. The translations have been printed as received, and each translator is only responsible for his own portion of the work. In the short introduction placed at the head of each, will be found a notice of where the text exists, and has been published, and if it has been previously translated; but no philological exegesis has been given. Owing to the discrepancies and difficulties which are attendant on the different systems of chronology, it has not been deemed advisable to give the exact dates B.C. of the documents, but an indication of general period to which each belongs is denoted by the title or heading. The nature of each monument is also mentioned, whether it is inscribed on stone, or a tablet, or cylinder of terra cotta, or object of other material employed for the purpose.

The form of the cuneiform characters varied considerably, according to age, locality, and the hand of the script in which it was inscribed, the oldest mounting to the earliest age of the Babylonian and Assyrian monarchies; this style of writing not having been entirely discontinued at the commencement of the Roman empire.

It has not been possible to arrange the materials in chronological order, but the list appended of the known texts and monuments, will convey to the reader some idea of their relative age, and extent of the literature, of Babylon, Assyria, Egypt, and other Eastern nations of antiquity.

S. BIRCH.

London, December 25, 1873.

CONTENTS.

INSCRIPTION

OF

RIMMON-NIRARI.

TRANSLATED BY

REV. A. H. SAYCE, M.A.

———————

THE following Inscription is found upon a Pavement Slab from Nimrud, which was discovered at the edge of the mound between the North-West and South-West Palaces. A lithographed copy of it is contained in the first volume of the "Cuneiform Inscriptions of Western Asia," p. 35, No. 3. The first 25 lines were originally published in the volume of Cuneiform Inscriptions edited by Mr. Layard, p. 70, With

2

the exception of the last 6 lines, the Inscription was printed

in Bonomi's popular work on Nineveh, p. 339. Its genea-

logical value is great, and it contains a notice of the founder

of the Assyrian Monarchy who is otherwise unknown.

TRANSLATION OF THE INSCRIPTION.

1 The Palace of Rimmon-Nirari, the great king, the powerful king,

2 The mighty king, king of the land of Assyria, the king whom, as his own son, Assur

3 King of the Gods of Heaven has favoured and with the kingdom

4 Of the *World* has filled

5 His hand. From the great sea

6 Of the Rising Sun[1] to the great sea

7 Of the Setting Sun[2]

8 His hand has conquered and ruled it

9 Wholly and throughout. The son of Samas-Rimmon,

10 The great king, the powerful king, the mighty king, king of the land of Assyria,

11 King of the *World*, son of Shalmaneser

12 King of the Four Races,[3] who on the land of his foes

13 Laid (his) yoke, and swept (them) like a whirlwind.

14 Grandson of Assur-natsir-pal, the warrior priest,

15 The enlarger of glorious habitations.

16 Rimmon-nirari, the glorious prince, to whose help

17 The gods Assur, Samas (the Sun), Rimmon, and Merodach

18 Have gone, and have enlarged his country

19 (Is) the descendant of the grandson of Tiglath-Adar,[4] king of Assyria,

[1] That is either the Persian Gulf or the Caspian Sea.
[2] The Mediterranean.
[3] The Four Races was an old title of Syria, which was peopled, according to Gen. x. 23, by Uz and Hul and Gether and Mash.
[4] He was the father of Assur-natsir-pal.

20 King of the country of Sumeri and Accad,[1]
21 Descendant[2] of Shalmaneser, the powerful king,
22 The erecter of the Temple of Kharsak-Kurra,[3]
23 The mountain of the world ; descendant
24 Of Bel-sumili-capi, a former king
25 Who went before (me), the founder of the monarchy,
26 Of which for its exaltation from
27 Ancient times Assur has proclaimed the glory.

[1] This denoted Babylonia. Sumeri is perhaps the Shinar of Scripture.
[2] Literally "offspring of the offspring."
[3] This signifies "the mountains of the East," that is to say, the high-lands of Elam from which the Accadai or "Highlanders" had originally descended.

THE

INSCRIPTION OF KHAMMURABI.

TRANSLATED BY

H. F. TALBOT, F.R.S., ETC.

THIS inscription is valuable from its extreme antiquity. Khammurabi lived before the time of Moses, but how many centuries earlier has not yet been ascertained. His inscriptions are, with one exception, written in the Accadian language which as yet is very imperfectly understood.

Very fortunately the Museum at Paris possesses one inscription written in the Babylonian language, and this is the one of which I have here given the translation. It was first translated by Oppert and Ménant, and afterwards M. Ménant wrote a special work on the subject, entitled *Inscriptions de Hammourabi roi de Babylone, traduites et publiées avec un commentaire à l'appui par M. Joachim Ménant* (Paris 1863). This work is accompanied by facsimiles of the inscriptions. I published a version of the inscription in 1863 in the Journal of the Royal Asiatic Society, vol. 20 p. 445 and a somewhat better one in 1865, aided by the facsimile, in the Transactions of the Royal Society of Literature, vol. 8, p. 234.

The great importance of this inscription resides, not in the events treated of, but in the language itself: for, we have here the proof that the Babylonian language was the same in the days of Khammurabi as it was a thousand years later in the days of Nebuchadnezzar. There are a few archaisms but they are very trifling. The amount of difference is perhaps as much as exists between the English of Queen Elizabeth's time and that of the present day. How far then must we recede into antiquity, if we wish to find the *beginnings* of the Semitic tongue! In all the inscriptions which have come down to us we find substantially the same language.

Other languages, and totally different ones, existed at the same time, of which the most important was the *Accadian*, in which the greater number of Khammurabi's inscriptions are written. That monarch evidently ruled over two races, which lived side by side, or perhaps intermixed, in ancient Babylonia.

TRANSLATION OF

THE INSCRIPTION.

COLUMN I.

Khammurabi the exalted king, the king of Babylon, the king renowned throughout the world : conqueror of the enemies of Marduk : the king beloved by his heart, am I.

The favour of God and Bel the people of Sumir and Accad gave unto my government. Their celestial weapons unto my hand they gave.

The canal Khammurabi, the joy of men, a stream of abundant waters, for the people of Sumir and Accad I excavated. Its banks, all of them, I restored to newness : new supporting walls I heaped up : perennial waters for the people of Sumir and Accad I provided.

COLUMN II.

The people of Sumir and Accad, all of them, in general assemblies I assembled. A review and inspection of them I ordained every year. In joy and abundance I watched over them, and in peaceful dwellings I caused them to dwell.

By the divine favour I am Khammurabi the exalted king, the worshipper of the supreme deity.

With the prosperous power which Marduk gave me, I built a lofty Citadel, on a high mound of earth, whose summits rose up like mountains, on the bank of Khammurabi river, the joy of men.

To that Citadel I gave the name of the mother who bore me [1] and the father who begot me.

In the holy name of Ri the mother who bore me, and of the father who begot me, during long ages may it last!

---

[1] He named it the fortress of Ri-Marduk, the god and goddess whom he called his father and mother, according to a fantastic custom of which the inscriptions offer many examples.

MONOLITH
INSCRIPTION OF SAMAS-RIMMON.

TRANSLATED BY

REV. A. H. SAYCE, M.A.

THE Inscription translated below is engraved upon an Obelisk found in the South-East Palace of Nimrud, the ancient Calah, and now in the British Museum. It is written in archaic characters, which differ greatly from those ordinarily met with on the Assyrian monuments. They are more picturesque than the latter, and were therefore sometimes preferred for the same reason that makes us occasionally adopt the old black-letter type. The Inscription is given in the First Volume of the " Cuneiform Inscriptions of Western Asia," edited by Sir H. Rawlinson and Mr. Norris in 1861, pp. 29-34. It has already been translated by Dr. Oppert in his " Histoire des Empires de Chaldée et d'Assyrie d'apres les monuments" (1865); but the present Translation is the first that has been made into English. Shalmaneser, the father of the king who had the Inscription engraved, was one of the greatest monarchs of the Middle Assyrian Empire. He reigned 35 years, and was a cotemporary of the Israelite

kings Ahab and Jehu, and of Hazael of Syria. Ahab is
mentioned in an Inscription which Shalmaneser caused to
be set up at Kurkh, and the names of Jehu and Hazae
occur on an Obelisk of Black Marble, adorned with sculptures of tribute-bearers, which occupies a conspicuous place
in the British Museum. The reign of Samas-Rimmon
lasted 13 years; and the inscription itself gives an account
of his successful suppression of a revolt raised by his brother
Assur-dayan, which, like that of Adonijah, threatened to
deprive Samas-Rimmon of the crown that had been destined
for him.

TRANSLATION OF THE INSCRIPTION.

COLUMN I.

1 To Adar,[1] the courageous lord

2 of mighty *chiefs*, the lord,

3 the hero of the gods, the roller of the globe of heaven

4 and earth, the urger on of all,

5 the supporter of the Deities of Heaven (and) of rain-storms,

6 the *bright one*, whose powers

7 are unequalled, chief of the Annunaci,[2]

8 the most powerful of the gods, the *oracle*,

9 the high *ruler* of the Southern Sun,

10 Lord over the force of the whirlwind,

11 who, like the destroying sun, the threshhold of the gods

12 crosses, and the regions of the *leaders*

13 of the gods, who *diffuse* glory,

14 fills with the abundance of all powers,

15 (and) the strength (of them); First-born of Bel, the servant

16 of the gods, his superiors, offspring of Beth-Eser,[3] the son

---

[1] The name of this god is variously read as Nin-ip, Bar, and Ussur.

[2] The Anunnaci, the offspring of Anu or the Sky, had their seat in the Lower world. They are called the Deities of the Earth.

[3] Beth-Eser, " The Temple of Uprightness," was the name given to the Temples of Adar.

17 the ruler, who among the fragments of broken diadems

18 launches the arrow, offspring of *Bit-Kur* (?), receiver of the instructions of

19 Anu and the Great Goddess, who change not

20 the utterance of his mouth,[1] the mighty chief, the supreme (one), the magnified,

21 Lord of the divine-powers, who the *sinews* of the hands and feet

22 binds together [and] brings the design to completion,

23 high among the gods, the lord who dwells in Calah,

24 the crown of perfect places,

25 the seat of the Southern Sun ;

26 Samas-Rimmon[2] the mighty king, king of multitudes

27 unequalled (in number), the shepherd of (sacred) places, bearer of the sceptre

28 of the shrines, the descender into all lands, the urger on

29 of all . . . . . whom from former days

30 the gods have called by name, the protector, the restorer

31 of Beth-Eser he who transgresses not, the roller of the front of Bit-Kur.

32 (As to) whom, for the embellishment of Bit-Kharsak-Kurra (and) the Temples[3] of his land

33 his heart is established and his ears exist ;

34 the son of Shalmaneser, the king of the Four Races,

35 the opponent of kings of all (countries), the trampler on the world,

36 the grandson of Assur-natsir-pal

37 the receiver of the tribute

38 and the riches of all regions.

[1] Or " the utterance of whose mouth shall never be changed."

[2] Samas is the Sun-god. Rimmon is the god of the atmosphere, whose name has been variously read Iva, Ao, Vul, and Bin.

[3] The word used here is the Plural of Bit-kur which literally signifies Temple of the Country."

39 It came to pass that Assur-dayin, the son, in the time of Shalmaneser

40 his father, made war. The overthrow of fealty wickedly

41 he brought about and caused the country to rebel, and made ready

42 battle. The men of the country of Assyria above and below with him

43 he collected, and he fortified the habitable towns. The cities he caused to be counted over, and

44 to make conflict and battle he set his face.

45 The cities of Nisura, Adia, Sibaniba, Imgur-Bel,[1] Issabri,

46 Beth-Imdira, Simu, Sibkhinis, Parnusur, Kipsuna,

47 Kurban, Tidu, Napulu, Capa, Assur,[2] Huracca,

48 Sallad (?), Khuzirina, Dur-baladh,[3] Dariga, Zab,

49 Lubdu, Arapkha,[4] Arbela, as far as Amida, Tel-Abni,[5] (and)

50 Khin-makhnu, in all 27 fortified towns with their citadels, which from

51 Shalmaneser, king of the Four Races, my father, had revolted (and)

52 on the side of Assur-dayan, the son, had ranged themselves, by the will of the great gods, my lords,

53 my feet I made them kiss in my first campaign, when to the country of Nahri[6]   *(Continued on Column II.)*

---

[1] Imgur-Bel was the name of the walls of Babylon.

[2] Assur, the original capital of Assyria, is the modern Kalah-Shergat.

[3] This means "The Fortress of Life."

[4] The name of the city has hitherto been read in this way, and the classical Arrapachitis compared with it. It ought, however, to be either *Sanakha* or *Arbanun.*

[5] That is "The Mound of Stones."

[6] Literally "The Country of Rivers." It corresponds with Northern Mesopotamia, the Aram Naharaim of Scripture.

COLUMN II.

1 I went up. Tribute (in the shape of)
2 horses harnessed to the yoke
3 from all the kings of
4 Nahri I received at the same time.
5 The land of Nahri to its frontiers
6 like shavings I swept.
7 The border of Assyria, which (extended) from the city
of Paddira
8 in Nahri as far as
9 Kar-Shalmaneser, near
10 Carchemish, from the country of Zaddi,
11 the border of Accad, as far as
12 Enzi, from the country of Aridi as far as
13 the country of the Sukhi, by the will of Assur, Samas,
14 Rimmon, (and) Istar, the gods, my protectors,
15 *with shame of face*, my feet
16 kissed. In my second campaign
17 Mulis-Assur, chief of the commanders,
18 a leader skilful in fighting, a man of authority,[1]
19 with my war-engines and my camp
20 to Nahri I urged on, and
21 sent it forth. Unto the sea of the setting sun he
went.
22 Three hundred cities
23 of Khirtsina, the son
24 of Migdi-ara (and) eleven fortresses
25 as well as 200 cities
26 of Uspina he cut off; their fighting men
27 he slew; their spoil, their treasure, their goods,
28 their gods, their sons, (and) their daughters
29 he carried off; their cities he threw down,

[1] Literally "man of command."

30 dug up (and) burned with fire. On his return

31 the fighting men of the country of the Sunbai he slaughtered.

32 A multitude of horses, trained

33 (to) the yoke, belonging to the kings of Nahri,

34 all of them I received. In my third campaign the river Zab

35 I crossed. The country of Tsilar I passed through.

36 To the land of Nahri I went up. The tribute

37 of Dadi of the country of the Khupuscai,[1]

38 of Khirtsina, the son of Migdi-ara,

39 of the country of the Sunbai, (of) the country of the Manai,[2]

40 (of) the country of the Parsuai (and of) the country of the Taurlai,

41 (namely) horses trained (to) the yoke,

42 I received. (As to) the country of the Mi'sai, exceeding fear

43 of Assur my lord overwhelmed them.

44 Before the brightness of my mighty arrows

45 they had fear, and their cities they abandoned.

46 A mountain difficult (of access) they occupied.

47 Three mountain peaks, which like the mist

48 reached unto heaven, over which no bird

49 could find its passage,[3] the place

50 as their stronghold they made.[4] After them I rode.

51 At those mountain peaks I arrived.

52 In a single day like an eagle over them I rushed.

---

[1] Khupusca lay to the North-East of Assyria, among the mountains of Armenia.

[2] The Manai or Mannai, called Minni in the Old Testament, inhabited the neighbourhood of Lake Van in Armenia.

[3] Literally "which a bird his crossing came not (to)."

[4] Literally "the place of them (i. e. the mountain-peaks) for their stronghold they made."

53 Multitudes of their soldiers I slew : their spoil,

54 their treasure, their goods, their oxen, their asses,

55 their sheep, horses trained (to) the yoke,

56 bulls which (have) two humps[1]

57 (and) horns to a countless number from the midst of the mountains I caused to be brought down.

58 Five hundred cities which (were) dependent upon them I threw down, dug up,

59 (and) burned with fire.   To the country of Girubbunda[2]

(Continued on Column III.)

---

[1] *I. e.* Camels.

[2] Girubbunda lay to the east of the Par'suai, who are probably the Parthians, and to the west of the Medes, at that time considerably eastward of the country afterwards called after their name.

COLUMN III.

1 I went. The city of Cinaci I cut off,

2 threw down, dug up (and) burned with fire.

3 The country that belonged to Nirisbizida

4 I passed through. The tribute of Titamasca

5 of the city of the Samasai, (and of) Ci-ara of the city of the Kar-'sibutai,

6 (namely) horses trained (to) the yoke, I received.

7 (As to) the country of Girubbunda, all its inhabitants the fear of my lordship

8 and the onset of my mighty battle overwhelmed, and

9 their cities they abandoned. To

10 the city Huras, their fortified stronghold, I went down ; and

11 this city I besieged, I captured. The corpses

12 of their warriors, like rubbish I scattered. Their city

13 I laid in heaps ; 600 of their warriors I slew.

14 Pirisati their king, with 1,200 of his fighting men

15 into bondage I took. Their spoil, their treasure, their goods,

16 their oxen, their sheep, their horses, property

17 (in) silver, (and) gold mingled with bronze, to

18 a countless amount, I carried off. I pulled down, dug up

19 (and) burned with fire. The tribute of Engur

20 of the city of the Tsibarai I received. An image

21 of my magnified royalty I made.[1] The laws

22 of Assur my lord, the decrees of my ascendancy

23 and the full history of the deeds of my hand, which in

24 the country of Nahri I wrought, upon it

25 I wrote. Into the city of Tsibara,

26 their fortified stronghold in the country of the Girubbundai,

[1] That is, he had a statue of himself erected.

3

27 I caused (it) to be brought.   To the country of the Matai[1] I went.

28 Before the mighty arrows of Assur, and the trial

29 of my terrible battle, which had not rest,

30 they had fear ; and their cities they abandoned.

31 To the country of Epitse after them

32 I rode : 2,300 soldiers of Khanatsiruca

33 of the country of the Matai I slew; 140 of his war-carriages

34 I seized.   His treasure his goods to a countless amount

35 I brought back to the city Sagbita, the capital. As many as

36 1,200 of his cities I threw down, dug up, (and) burned with fire.

37 On my return the passes of the mountains I made my way through.

38 Munir'suarta of the country of the Araziasai,[2] together with

39 1,070 of his fighting-men with arrows I slaughtered.

40 (With) their corpses the successive valleys of the high country

41 I filled : their sons, their daughters, their treasure,

42 their goods, their oxen, (and) their sheep the armies

43 of my country as tribute carried away.   Their cities I threw down,

44 dug up (and) burned with fire.   At that time the tribute

45 of Sirasmi of the country of the Babarurai, of Amakhar

46 of the city of the Kharmis-andai, of Zarisu of the country of the Par'saniyai,

47 of Zarisu of the city of the Khundurai, of Sanisu

48 of the country of the Cipabarutacai, of Ardara

40 of the country of the Ustassai, of Suma of the country of the Cinucai,

---

[1] These are the Medes.

[2] The Araziasians are placed by Lenormant in Sagartia.

50 of Tatai of the country of the Ginginai,

51 of Bi'sirain of the country of the Arimai, of Parusta

52 of the country of the Cimarusai, of Aspastatauk

53 of the Huilai, of Amamas of the country of the Cingistilinzakharai[1]

54 of Kha's'sikhu of the country of the Matsirausai, of Mamanis

55 of the country of the Luk'sai, of Zabel of the country of the Dimamai,

56 of Sirasu of the country of the 'Singuriai, of Gista

57 of the country of the Abdanai, of Adadanu of the country of the A'satai,

58 of Ur'si of the country of the Ginkhukhtai, of Bara

59 of the country of the Ginzinai, of Arua of the country of the Cindutausai,

60 of Dirnacus of the country of the Marruai, of Zabanu

61 of the country of the Zuzarurai, of Irtizati of the country of the Ginkhidai

62 of Bazzuta of the country of the Taurlai, of Sua

63 of the country of the Nanikirians (?), of 'Satiriai, (and) of Arta'sirari

64 kings of the country of Nahri all of them, by the will of Assur, Samas,

65 (and) Rimmon, the gods my defenders, a fixed tribute

66 of horses trained (to) the yoke for the future

67 over them I appointed. At that time from the country of Tsilar

68 (and) the land of Edanni as far as the sea of the setting sun, like Rimmon,

69 my storm over them I poured. Exceeding fear

70 into them I infused. In my fourth campaign, (in the month) Sivan[2] (Continued on Column IV.)

---

[1] The latter part of this word seems to be the Assyrian *Zakharu* "small."

[2] Sivan, the 3rd month of the year, answered roughly to our May.

COLUMN IV.

1 (on) the 15th day to Car-Duniyas[1] (my troops) go, and

2 the river Zab I crossed. Between the cities of Zaddi and Zaba

3 fragments of rock I passed. Three fierce lions I slew.

4 The country of Ebikh I passed through. The city of the waters of the Dhurnat[2] I approached.

5 Exceeding fear of Assur and Merodach, the great gods,

6 my lords, overwhelmed them. My feet they took.[3] These men

7 I caused to go out, and with their goods (and) their gods to the midst

8 of my own country I brought them. As men of my own country I counted (them).

9 The Dhurnat I crossed in its upper part.[4] The city Karne,

10 the capital of the country,[5] as well as 200 towns dependent upon it I threw down, [dug up]

11 (and) burned with fire. The country of Yalman I passed through. The city Diahbina

12 I approached. The fear of Assur overwhelmed the inhabitants. My feet they took.

13 Three thousand cities with their men, their treasure (?) their goods, from the midst

14 of that city I took. The cities of Datebir (and) Iz . . . ya

15 which (are) beside the city Ganasuticanu, together with 200 cities

[1] Car-duniyas was the name usually given to Lower Chaldea.
[2] This river is the Tornadotus of classical geographers.
[3] As a token of homage and submission.
[4] Or "in its flood."
[5] Literally, "its royal city."

16 that (are) dependent on them I conquered : 330 of their soldiers I slew :

17 Their spoil, their treasure, their goods, (and) their gods I carried off : their plantation

18 I cut down : their towns I threw down, dug up, (and) burned with fire. The men who from the face

19 of my mighty arrows fled, into a city in the midst of (their other) cities, their fortified (stronghold,)

20 entered.   That city I besieged, I captured.   Five hundred of their soldiers I slew.   Their spoil,

21 their treasure, their goods, their gods, their oxen (and) their sheep I carried off.   The city

22 I threw down, dug up, (and) burned with fire.   As to all the land of Accad, which before the fear

23 of my terrible arrows (and) the trial of my mighty battle, which cessation had not,

24 had fear, and into the city of Dur-Papsukul (?) the capital, which like a crag in the river

25 in a flood of waters was situated [so that] for the attack of my army

26 it [was] not good, (and into) 447 cities round about (it) had entered,

27 that city in my passage I captured.   Thirteen thousand

28 of its fighting-men with arrows I slew.   Their dead bodies

29 like water I scattered.   Their city I demolished.   The ranks

30 of their warriors into heaps I heaped.

31 Three thousand lives with a measuring-line I took : its royal divan, the treasures of its palace,

32 the guards of its high altar, the amazons of its high altars, its stores,

33 its goods, its gods, the . . . . . of its high altar, to a countless number,

34 from the midst of that town I carried off.   The ranks of its warriors,

35 like flocks of birds,[1] to the armies of my country

36 yielded.   That city I pulled down, dug up (and) burned with fire.

37 Merodach-baladhsu-ikbi to the strength of his troops

38 trusted, and the country of Chaldæa, the country of Elam, the country of Zimri,

39 (and) the country of Arumu, with their numerous troops to a countless amount,

40 summoned together.   To make conflict and battle against me he came.

41 Over against Ahdaban, in the neighbourhood of the city of Dur-Papsukul (?) a fortified town,

42 where he marshalled his troops, with him I fought. A destruction of him I made.

43 Five thousand of the ranks of (his) men I destroyed. Two thousand lives in the hands I took.

44 One hundred of his chariots, 200 of his war-carriages, his royal pavilion, (his) divan, (and)

45 his camp I seized.

---

[1] I think a character has fallen out of the text here.   Otherwise we must translate (with Norris) "as if by destiny."

THE

INSCRIPTION ON BELLINO'S CYLINDER,

COMPRISING THE FIRST TWO YEARS OF THE

REIGN OF SENNACHERIB.

TRANSLATED BY

H. F. TALBOT, F.R.S., ETC.

———————

THIS inscription is preserved in the British Museum. It was published, by Layard, in the first volume of the British Museum Inscriptions, plate 63.

An admirable facsimile of it was made by Bellino, and engraved by the care of Grotefend, in "*Abhandlung der k. Ges. d. Wissensch, zu Göttingen.*"

In 1866 I presented a translation of it to the Royal Society of Literature, which is printed in their Transactions (vol. viii. p. 369).[1]

---

[1] I had made a previous attempt in 1860 (Journal of the Royal Asiatic Society, vol. xviii. p. 76).

TRANSLATION OF THE INSCRIPTION.

Line 1 Sixty-three inscribed lines: (*written*) in the seventh month of the year whose *eponym* was Nebo-liha, prefect of Arbela.

---

2 SENNACHERIB, the great king, the powerful king, the king of Assyria, the king unrivalled, the pious monarch, the worshipper of the great gods.

3 The protector of the just: the lover of the righteous:
. . . . .¹

4 The noble warrior, the valiant hero, the first of all kings, the great punisher of unbelievers, who are breakers of the holy festivals.

5 Ashur, the great Lord, has given to me an unrivalled monarchy. Over all princes he has raised triumphantly my arms.

6 In the beginning of my reign I defeated Marduk Baladan, king of Babylonia, and his allies the Elamites, in the plains near the city of Kish.

7 In the midst of that battle he quitted his camp, and fled alone: he escaped to the city of Gutzumman: he got into the marshes full of reeds and rushes, and so saved his life.

8 The chariots, waggons, horses, mules, camels, and dromedaries, which in the midst of the battle he had abandoned, were captured by my hands.

9 I entered rejoicing into his palace in the city of Babylon: I broke open his royal treasury: gold and silver: vessels of gold and silver: precious stones of every kind: goods and valuables, and much royal treasure,

¹ Some words here follow, in praise of the king, whose meaning is uncertain.

10 his wife : the men and women of his palace : the noblemen : and those who ranked first among all his men of trust, and were clothed with the chief authority in the palace, I carried off, and I counted them as a spoil.

11 I marched after him to the city Gutzumman, and I sent off my soldiers to search through the marshes and reeds. Five days they moved about rapidly, but his hiding place was not discovered !

12 In the power of Ashur, my lord, 89 large cities, and royal dwellings in the land of Chaldea, and 820 small towns in their neighbourhood I assaulted, captured, and carried off their spoils.

13 The Urbi [*Arabians*], Aramæans, and Chaldæans who were in the cities of Erech, Nipur, Kish, Harris-kalama, and Tiggaba, and the people of the cities which had been in rebellion I carried away, and I distributed them as a spoil.

14 Belibus, the son of a *Rabbani*, who was prefect (?) of Suanna[1] city, who as a young man had been brought up in my palace, I placed over them as king of Leshan and Akkadi.

15 During my return, the tribes of the Tuhamuna, Rihi-khu, Yadakku, Hubudu, Kipri, Malikhu, Gurumu, Hubuli, Damunu,

16 Gambulu, Khindaru, Ruhuha, Bukudu, Khamranu, Hagaranu, Nabatu, and Lihutahu (Aramæans all of them, and rebels), I completely conquered.

17 208,000 people, male and female : 7,200 horses and mules; 11,173 asses; 5,230 camels; 80,100 oxen; 800,600 sheep ; a vast spoil, I carried off to Assyria.

18 In the course of my expedition I received the great tribute of Nebo-bil-zikri, chief of Ararat : gold, silver, meshukan wood of great size, mules, camels, oxen and sheep.

---

[1] Suanna was the name of a part of Babylon, accounted sacred.

19 The people of the city Khirimmi, obstinate enemies, who from old times had never bowed down to my yoke, I destroyed with the sword. Not one soul escaped.

20 That district I settled again. One ox, ten sheep, ten goats (?) (these twenty beasts being the best of every kind), I appointed [*as a sacrifice*] to the gods of Assyria, my lords, in every township.[1]

21 In my second expedition, Ashur, the lord, giving me confidence, I marched against the land of the Kassi and Yatsubi-galla,[2] obstinate enemies, who from old times had never submitted to the kings, my fathers.

22 Through the thick forests and in the hilly districts I rode on horseback, for I had left my two-horse chariot in the plains below. But in dangerous places I alighted on my feet, and clambered like a mountain goat.

23 The city of Beth-Kilamzakh, their great city, I attacked and took. The inhabitants, small and great, horses, mules, asses, oxen, and sheep, I carried off from it and distributed them as a spoil.

24 Their smaller towns without number I overthrew, and reduced them to heaps of rubbish. A vast building, which was their Hall of Assembly, I burnt with fire, and left it in ruins.

25 I rebuilt that city of Beth-Kilamzakh, and I made it into a strong fortress. Beyond former times I strengthened it and fortified it. People drawn from lands subdued by my arms I placed to dwell within it.

26 The people of Kassi and Yatsubi-galla, who had fled away from my arms, I brought down from the mountains, and in the cities of Kar-Thisbe and Beth-Kubitti I caused them to dwell.

---

[1] Into the conquered country he introduced the Assyrian worship, and of course made due provision for the support of the priests, and sacrifices to the gods.

[2] *I. e.* 'Men of great stature.'—Name of a tribe.

27 In the hands of my general, the prefect of Arrapkha, I placed them. A stone tablet I made : I wrote on it the victories which I had gained over them, and within the city I set it up.

28 Then I turned round the front of my chariot, and I took the road to the land of Illipi. Before me Ispabara their king abandoned his strong cities, and his treasuries, and fled to a distance.

29 All his broad country I swept like a mighty whirlwind. The city Marupishti, and the city Akkudu, his royal residences, and 34 great cities, with numberless smaller towns in their neighbourhood,

30 I ravaged, destroyed, and burnt them with fire. I cut down their woods. Over their corn fields I sowed thistles. In every direction I left the land of Illipi a desert.

31 The inhabitants, small and great, male and female, horses, mules, asses, oxen, and sheep beyond number, I carried off, and sent them away until none were left.

32 The strong cities of Sisirta and Kummakhli, and the smaller towns in their neighbourhood, together with the whole province of Beth-Barrua, I cut off from his land, and added them to the empire of Assyria.

33 I established the city of Ilinzash to be the royal city and metropolis of that province. I abolished its former name, and I gave it the name of the city of Sennacherib.

34 During my return I received a great tribute from the distant Medians, who, in the days of the kings, my fathers, no one had ever heard even the name of their country ; and I made them bow down to the yoke of my majesty.

35 In those days, Niniveh, the exalted city, the city beloved by Ishtar : within which dwells the worship of all the gods and goddesses,

36 The ancient *timin*[1] of its palace, those of old time had stamped its clay with *sacred* (?) writing, and repeated it in the companion-tablets.

37 A splendid place, a storehouse of every kind, and a treasury for all their jewels and regalia, they erected within it.

38 Of all the kings of former days, my fathers who went before me, who reigned before me over Assyria, and governed the city of Bel (*i. e.* Niniveh),

39 And every year without fail augmented its interior rooms, and treasured up in them all their revenues which they received from the four countries,

40 Not one among them all, though the central palace was too small to be their royal residence, had the knowledge, nor the wish to improve it.

41 As to caring for the health of the city, by bringing streams of water into it, and the finding of new springs, none turned his thoughts to it, nor brought his heart to it.

42 Then I, Sennacherib, king of Assyria, by command of the gods, resolved in my mind to complete this work, and I brought my heart to it.

43 Men of Chaldæa, Aram, Manna, Kue, and Cilicia, who had not bowed down to my yoke, I brought away as captives, and I compelled them to make bricks.

44 In baskets made of reeds which I cut in the land of Chaldæa, I made the foreign workmen bring their appointed tale of bricks, in order to complete this work.

45 The former palace, of 360 measures long, adjoining the gardens of the Great Tower : 80 measures wide, adjoining the watchtower of the temple of Ishtar : 134 measures wide,

[1] The *timin* was the clay tablet or cylinder deposited in the foundation stone, or sometimes at the four corners of a building. It was regarded with peculiar reverence. So the Hebrews appear to have regarded the "corner stone." It was intended to remain for ever. If found by a subsequent king, it was to be read with reverence, and restored to its former place.

adjoining the watchtower of the house of worship : and
95 measures wide, ... [1]

46 Which the kings, my fathers, who went before me had
built for their royal residence, but had not beautified its
front.

47 The river Tibilti[2] had ruined the brickwork of it when
it ravaged the quays of the central city.[3] The trees of its
gardens had been burnt for firewood years ago.

48 For a long time this river had undermined the front
of the palace. In the high water of its floods it had made
great rents in the foundations, and had washed away the
timin.

49 That small palace I pulled down, the whole of it. I
made a new channel for the river Tibilti, I regulated its
water, I restrained its flow.

50 Within its old limits I walled up its stream. The low
platform[4] I raised higher, and paved it firmly with stones of
great size, covered with bitumen, for a space of 354 measures
in length, and 279 in breadth.[5] That space I elevated
above the waters, and restored it to be again dry ground.

51 1700 measures long : 162 measures wide, on the
upper side towards the north : 217 measures wide in the
centre,

[1] The scribe has left this line unfinished, from its length, notwithstanding
that he wrote the letters as close together as possible. He might have
continued it in the following line, but would not do so. This is a clear
proof that the sense was sometimes sacrificed to beauty of writing.
[2] Perhaps another name for the Tigris, meaning "The Stream of Fer-
tility." Most of the rivers appear to have had fanciful or poetical names,
a list of which is given in 2 R, plate 51. We there read that the Euphrates
was called, "Life of the Land ;" and the Tigris, "Babilat Nukhsi," or
"Stream of Gladness," etc., etc.
[3] The old palace is called in the Bull inscription, "The Palace of the
Central City." See 3 R, 13, line 4 of the second column.
[4] The old palace being pulled down, its platform remained, but so low
as to be nearly on a level with the neighbouring river.
[5] This measurement is added from another account (Layard's Inscriptions, plate 38, line 16, confirmed by the Bull inscription, Layard, plate 62,
line 23).

52 386 measures wide, on the lower side towards the south, fronting the river Tigris, I completed the mound, and I measured the measure.

53 The *timin* of old times had not been forgotten, owing to the veneration of the people.[1] With a layer of large stones I enclosed its place, and I made its deposit secure.

54 The written records of my name, 160 fathoms of bas-reliefs, I sculptured in the palace, but the lower part of the wall, next to the ground, I left to be filled up in future times.

55 Afterwards I resolved to have more tablets carved. I sculptured twenty fathoms of them in addition to the former ones, so that I formed 180 fathoms of them altogether.

56 The enclosure itself I increased beyond what it was in former days : above the measure of the former palace I enlarged it, and I liberally augmented its dwellings,[2]

57 And its fine buildings of ivory, *dan* wood, *ku* wood, *meshukan* wood, cedar wood, cypress wood, and pistachio wood. And in the midst I placed my royal residence, the palace of ZAKDI̅ NU ISHA.[3]

58 Around it I planted the finest of trees, equal to those of the land of Khamana, which all the knowing prefer to those of the land of Chaldæa.

59 By my care I caused the uprising of springs in more than forty places in the plain : I divided them into irrigating canals for the people of Niniveh, and gave them to be their own property.

---

[1] This does not seem to contradict what was said before (line 48) that the old *timin* was washed away: for its memory may have survived in the traditions of the people, and a new copy may have been deposited in the platform of Sennacherib's palace.

[2] The palace enclosure contained many separate buildings, appropriated to various uses, and some of them were, perhaps, the dwellings of the great officers of state.

[3] *I. e.* HAS NOT AN EQUAL.

60 To obtain water to turn the flour mills, I brought it in pipes from Kishri to Niniveh, and I skilfully constructed water-wheels.

61 I brought down the perennial waters of the river Kutzuru,[1] from the distance of half a *Kasbu*,[2] into those reservoirs, and I covered them well.[3]

62 Of Niniveh, my royal city, I greatly enlarged the dwellings. Its streets, I renovated the old ones, and I widened those which were too narrow. I made them as splendid as the sun.

63 In future days, if one of the kings, my sons, whom Ashur shall call to the sovereignty over this land and people ; when this palace shall grow old and decay,

64 Shall repair its injuries, shall see the written record of my name, shall raise an altar, and sacrifice a male victim, and shall then replace it in its place : Ashur will hear and accept his prayers.

---

[1] Still called the Khausser.   [2] Three miles and a half.

[3] In the East it is essential to keep wells covered.

INSCRIPTION OF SENNACHERIB:

CONTAINING

THE ANNALS OF THE FIRST EIGHT
YEARS OF HIS REIGN.

FROM

AN HEXAGONAL CLAY PRISM FOUND AT NINIVEH IN 1830,

AND NOW IN THE BRITISH MUSEUM.

PUBLISHED in the first volume of Sir H. Rawlinson's British Museum inscriptions, plates 37 to 42. I presented a translation of it to the Royal Asiatic Society in October 1859, which was published in their Journal, vol. xix, p. 135. I have understood that a translation has since been published in France by M. Oppert, but I have not seen it.

I commence the present translation with the *Third Campaign*, the war with Hezekiah, because the history of the

4

first two campaigns is the same as on the Bellino Cylinder which I have already translated in this volume. It is for the most part a *verbatim* copy of it, which therefore I need not give again. But since these two inscriptions were written at an interval of several years, and by different scribes, we see that yearly Annals must have been published by Authority, to which the scribes were expected closely to adhere.

One remarkable deviation however occurs. In the Bellino cylinder we read that Belibus, a young nobleman, was made King of Babylonia, but in the later Annals this is struck out. It is evident that Belibus had proved a failure.

This interesting inscription is usually called the Taylor cylinder, from the name of its former possessor.

TRANSLATION OF THE INSCRIPTION,

COLUMN II.

Line 34 IN my Third Campaign to the land of Syria I went.
35 Luliah[1] king of Sidon (for the fearful splendour
36 of my majesty had overwhelmed him) to a distant spot
37 in the midst of the sea fled. His land I entered.
38 Sidon the greater, Sidon the lesser,
39 Beth-Zitti,[2] Sarepta, Makalliba,
40 Usu, Akziba,[3] Akku,[4]
41 his strong cities, and castles, walled
42 and fenced ; and his finest towns (for the flash of the weapons
43 of Ashur my lord had overcome them) made submission
44 at my feet. Tubaal upon the throne
45 over them I seated. A fixed tribute to my Majesty,
46 paid yearly without fail, I imposed upon him.
47 Then Menahem king of Ussimiruna
48 Tubaal king of Sidon
49 Abd-iliut king of Arvad
50 Uru-milki king of Gubal
51 Mitinti king of Ashdod
52 Buduel king of Beth-Ammon
53 Kammuz[5]-natbi king of Moab
54 Airammu[6] king of Edom

[1] Elulæus of classical authors.
[2] *I.e.*, the city of Olives.
[3] Achzib of Joshua xix. 29. Ecdippa of classical authors.
[4] Accho of the book of Judges i. 31. Akka of the Arabs. The modern St. Jean d'Acre.
[5] Kammuz (or Chemosh) was the chief god of the Moabites.
[6] Perhaps the same name as Hiram.

55 the kings of the west country, all of them . . . . . .

56 . . . . their great presents and wealth

57 to my presence brought, and kissed my feet.

58 And Zedek king of Ascalon

59 who had not bowed down to my yoke, the gods of his father's house, himself,

60 his wife, his sons, his daughters, his brothers, the race of his father's house

61 I carried off and brought them to Assyria.

62 Sarludari son of their former king Rukipti

63 over the men of Ascalon I placed ; a fixed gift

64 of offerings to my majesty I imposed on him . . . . .

65 In the course of my expedition, the cities of Beth-Dagon[1]

66 Joppa, Banai-barka[2] and Hazor,[3]

67 cities of Zedek, which to my feet

68 homage had not rendered, I attacked, captured, and carried off their spoils.

69 The chief priests, noblemen, and people of Ekron

70 who Padiah their king (holding the faith and worship

71 of Assyria) had placed in chains of iron, and unto Hezekiah

72 King of Judah had delivered him, and had acted towards the deity with hostility :

73 these men now were terrified in their hearts. The kings of Egypt

74 and the soldiers, archers, chariots, and horses of Ethiopia,

75 forces innumerable, gathered together and came

[1] Beth-Dagon in Judah is probably meant. Josh. xv. 41.

[2] Named in Joshua xix. 45.

[3] Hazor in Naphthali, Josh. xix. 36, seems too far north : perhaps Hazar Shual is meant.

76 to their assistance.   In the plains of Altaku[1]

77 in front of me they placed their battle array: they discharged

78 their arrows : with the weapons of Ashur my lord, with them

79 I fought, and I defeated them.

80 The chief of the chariots and the sons of the king of Egypt,

81 and the chief of the chariots of the king of Ethiopia, alive

82 in the midst of the battle my hands captured.   The city of Altaku

83 and the city of Tamna[2] I attacked captured and carried off their spoil.—

(Continued on Column III.*)*

[1] Eltekon of Josh. xv. 59.

[2] Timnah was in Judah near Ekron. Joshua xv. 10. Its name signifies "The South": it was near the south border of Palestine.

COLUMN III.

Line 1 THEN I drew nigh to the city of Ekron. The chief priests

2 and noblemen, who had committed these crimes, I put to death:

3 on stakes all round the city I hung their bodies:

4 the people of the city who had done likewise, together with their wives

5 to slavery I gave. The rest of them

6 who had not been guilty of faults and crimes, and who sinful things against the deity

7 had not done, to reward them I gave command. Padiah

8 their king from the midst of Jerusalem

9 I brought out, and on a throne of royalty over them

10 I seated. Tribute payable to my majesty

11 I fixed upon him. And Hezekiah

12 King of Judah, who had not bowed down at my feet

13 Forty six of his strong cities, his castles, and the smaller towns

14 in their neighbourhood beyond number

15 with warlike engines¹ . . . .

16 . . . .

17 I attacked and captured. 200,150 people small and great, male and female,

18 horses, mares, asses, camels, oxen

19 and sheep beyond number, from the midst of them I carried off

20 and distributed them as a spoil. He himself, like a bird in a cage, inside Jerusalem

21 his royal city I shut him up: siege-towers against him

---

¹ Several of these are named, but they cannot at present be identified.

22 I constructed. The exit of the great gate of his city, to divide it[1]

23 He had given command. His cities which I plundered, from his kingdom

24 I cut off, and to Mitinti king of Ashdod

25 Padiah king of Ekron, and Izmi-Bel

26 King of Gaza I gave them. I diminished his kingdom.

27 Beyond the former scale of their yearly gifts

28 their tribute and gifts to my majesty I augmented

29 and imposed them upon them. He himself Hezekiah

30 the fearful splendour of my majesty had overwhelmed him :

31 The workmen, soldiers, and builders

32 whom for the fortification of Jerusalem his royal city

33 he had collected within it, now carried tribute

34 and with thirty talents of gold, 800 talents of silver ; woven cloth,

35 scarlet, embroidered ; precious stones of large size ;

36 couches of ivory, moveable thrones of ivory, skins of *buffaloes*,

37 *teeth of buffaloes*, dan wood, ku wood, a great treasure of every kind,

38 and his daughters, and the male and female inmates of his palace, male *slaves*

39 and female *slaves*, unto Niniveh my royal city

40 after me he sent ; and to pay tribute

41 and do homage he sent his envoy.

---

42 IN my Fourth Campaign, Ashur my lord gave me confidence.

[1] "To divide, or unloose, what is chained together," is the sense of the term according to Fürst. It means, I think, that Hezekiah had commanded the drawbridge to be raised.

43 I assembled my numerous army : to the city of Beth-Yakina

44 to advance I gave command.   At the commencement of my expedition

45 of Suzubi the Chaldean, dwelling within the marshes

46 in the city Bittutu I accomplished the defeat.

47 He himself, for the fury of my attack overwhelmed him,

48 lost heart, and like a bird fled away alone

49 and his place of refuge could not be found.   I turned round the front of my chariot

50 and took the road to Beth-Yakina

51 He himself, Merodach-Baladan whom in the course

52 of my first campaign I had defeated

53 and had cut to pieces his army, the noise of my powerful arms

54 and the shock of my fiery battle he now fled from ;

55 The gods, rulers of his land, in their Arks he collected, and in ships

56 he transported them, and to the city of Nagiti-Rakkin

57 which is on the sea coast, like a bird he flew.   His brothers, the seed of his father's house

58 whom he had left on the seashore, and the rest of the people of his land

59 from Beth-Yakina within the marshes and morasses

60 I brought away and distributed them as slaves.   Once more his cities I destroyed

61 overthrew them and left them in heaps of ruins—To his protector

62 the king of Elam I caused terror—

63 On my return, Ashur-nadin-mu my eldest son,

64 brought up at my knees, I seated upon the throne of his kingdom :

65 all the land of Leshan and Akkad I entrusted to him.

---

66 In my Fifth Campaign the people of Tocharri

67 Sharum, Ezama, Kipsu, Kalbuda,

68 Kua and Kana, who like the nests of eagles

69 on the highest summits and wild crags of the Nipur mountains

70 had fixed their dwellings, refused to bow down to my yoke.

71 At the foot of Mount Nipur I pitched my camp:

72 with native guides who had kissed my feet [submitted]

73 and a band of my soldiers who were irregulars,

74 I, like the leader Bull, took the front of them.

75 In the . . . . . , in the mountain vallies, and through flooded lands

76 I travelled in my chariot: but in places which for my chariot were dangerous

77 I alighted on my feet; and like a mountain goat among the lofty cliffs

78 I clambered up them.   Where my knees

79 took rest, upon a mountain rock I sat down,

80 and water, cold even to freezing, to assuage my thirst I drank.

81 To the tops of the mountains I pursued them

82 and completely defeated them.   Their cities I captured;

(Continued on Column IV.)

COLUMN IV.

Line 1 I CARRIED off their spoils ; I ravaged, destroyed, and burnt them with fire.

2 Then I turned round the front of my chariot, and against Maniah

3 King of Ukku, chief of the rebellious Dahæ, I marched

4 by ways which had never been opened, lofty summits, where by reason of

5 the rocky mountains, no former king

6 had ever penetrated, of all those who reigned before me.

7 At the foot of Anara[1] and Uppa, fortified hills,

8 I pitched my camp ; but I myself in my travelling Chair

9 together with my light soldiery

10 into their narrow gorges with precaution I entered

11 and laboriously I climbed up to the tops of the high mountains.

12 He himself, Maniah, the multitude of my army

13 saw, and abandoned Ukku his royal city

14 and fled to a distance.   I besieged Ukku and captured it :

15 I carried off its spoils : every kind of goods and wealth,

16 the treasures of his palace, from the midst of it

17 I brought out and distributed them as a spoil.   And 33 cities

18 belonging to that province I captured.   Men, cattle,

19 oxen and sheep, from the midst of them

20 I carried off : and I ravaged, destroyed and burnt them with fire.

---

21 IN my Sixth Campaign, the rest of the men of Beth-Yakina

[1] Probably the Aornos of the Greeks, besieged long afterwards by Alexander the great.

22 who from before my powerful arms like birds

23 had fled away, the gods who rule over their land into their Arks

24 had collected, the great sea of the Rising Sun[1]

25 had crossed over, and in a city just opposite, in the land of Elam had placed

26 their dwellings. In Syrian ships I crossed the sea:

27 the cities of Nagitu, Nagitu-Dihubina, Khilmu,

28 Billatu, and Reshpan, cities of

29 Elam, I captured. The men of Beth-Yakina and their gods

30 and the men of Elam I carried away. Not even a remnant of them was left.

31 In ships I embarked them : to the other side

32 I caused them to cross : and I made them take the road to Assyria.

33 The cities in those provinces I ravaged, destroyed

34 and burnt with fire. I reduced them to ruins and rubbish.

35 In my return, Suzub the Babylonian

36 who to the sovereignty of the lands of Leshan and Accad

37 had restored himself, in a great battle

38 I defeated him, I captured him alive

39 strong chains of iron I placed on him : and to Assyria

40 I carried him off. The king of Elam who had encouraged him

41 and come to his assistance, I defeated

42 I dispersed his expedition and cut to pieces his army.

---

43 IN my Seventh Campaign, Ashur the lord gave me courage.

44 I advanced against Elam. The cities of Beth-Khairi

[1] The Persian Gulf.

45 and Raza, cities of the Assyrian empire

46 which, in the days of my father, the Elamite had seized by violence

47 in the course of my advance I captured and carried off their spoils:

48 soldiers devoted to me I placed within them

49 and restored them to the Assyrian empire.

50 In the hands of the governor of the fortress of Dur-el-ki I placed them

51 Then I destroyed the cities of Bubi, Dunni-Shemesh, Beth-Ritsiah,

52 Beth-Aklami, Duru, Kaltitsulaya,

53 Silibta, Beth-Assutsi, Kar-Mibasha,

54 Beth-Gitsi, Beth-Katpalani, Beth-Imbiah

55 Kamanu, Beth-Arrabi, Buruta,

56 Dinta-sha-Zuliah, Dinta-

57 sha-Antarbit-Karsa, Karrislaki, Rabaya,

58 Rassu, Akkabarina, Til-Ukhuri,

59 Kamran, Naditu, with the other cities of the gate (or entrance)

60 of Beth-Bunaki.　Til-Khumbi, Dinta-

61 sha-Dumian, Beth-Ubiah, Balti-lishir,

62 Tagab-lishir which is the city of the Nakindati,

63 Massut the lower, Sarkudiri, Zalisha-tarbit,

64 Beth-Akhi-adanna, and Iltimarba.　All these large cities, thirty-four in number

65 and smaller towns in their neighbourhood

66 beyond number, I attacked and captured, and carried off their spoils,

67 I ravaged, destroyed them, and burnt them with fire.

68 The smoke of their burning like a mighty cloud

69 obscured the face of high heaven.　When he heard of the capture

70 of his cities, Shadu-Nakhunda king of Elam was struck

71 with terror; into the rest of his cities he threw garrisons :

72 he himself abandoned Madakta his royal city

73 and towards Khaidala which is among high mountains

74 he took the road.   To the city Madakta, his royal city,

75 "Advance !" I commanded.   In the month of December a terrible storm

76 arrived, a vast cataract poured down,

77 rains upon rains, and snow, caused the torrents to burst forth.

78 Then I quitted the mountains.   I turned round the front of my chariot

79 and I took the road to Niniveh.   In those same days

80 by the will of Ashur my lord, Shadu-Nakhunda

(Continued on Column V.*)*

COLUMN V.

Line 1 king of Elam, did not complete three months [*more of life*]

2 on a day which was not fated for him[1] he was violently put to death.

3 After him Umman-Minan who was no friend to religion and law,

4 his brother *illegitimate,* sat upon his throne.

---

5 In my Eighth Campaign, after Suzub had escaped,

6 the children of Babylon, wicked devils,[2] the great gates of their city

7 hoisted up,[3] and hardened their hearts to make war—

8 Suzub the Chaldæan, Lidunnamu

9 a man who had no education, Kilpan prefect

10 of Lakhiri a refugee from Arrapkha,

11 and a band of dissolute men around him he assembled—

12 He entered among the marshes, and made there a hiding place :

13 then, to collect more men, he went back by himself

14 and passed into Elam, over the bounds and frontiers,

15 then, with the men and women who were with him

16 from Elam he returned rapidly, and entered the city of Suanna.[4]

17 The men of Babylon, in their folly, upon the throne

18 seated him, and the crown of Leshan and Accad bestowed upon him.

19 The treasury of the Great Temple they opened. The gold and silver

---

[1] *Viz.,* in the course of nature.   [2] This is a literal translation.
[3] Lifted the drawbridges.   [4] Suanna was the most sacred part of Babylon.

20 of Bel and Zarpanita and the wealth of their temples they brought out

21 and to Umman-Minan king of Elam who had

22 no right to it, they sent it as a bribe :

23 (saying) " Collect thy army ! strike thy camp !

24 " make haste to Babylon ! stand by our side !

25 " swear to help us !" Then he, the Elamite,

26 whom in the course of my former campaign into Elam

27 I had captured his cities and reduced them to ruins,

28 showed that he had no sense : he accepted the bribe.

29 He assembled his army in his camp. His chariots and waggons

30 he collected. Horses and mares he harnessed to their yokes :

31 the nations Parzush, Anzan, Pasiru, Illipi,

32 and the men of Yashan, Lakabri, Karzun,

33 Dummuku, Zulai, and the city of Samuna

34 (who was the son of Merodach Baladan); and the cities Beth-Adini, Beth-Amukkan,

35 Beth-Kutlan, Beth-Salatakki, Lakhiru,

36 Bukudu, Gambuli, Kalatu, Ruhua,

37 Ubuli, Malaku, Rapiku,

38 Khindaru and Damunu, a vast host of allies

39 he led along with him. They assembled themselves, and the road

40 to Babylonia they took. They rushed upon Babylon.

41 Unto Suzub the Chaldæan, king of Babylon

42 they approached and met him. They united their armies—

43 Then, as a mighty swarm of locusts[1] covers the face of the earth

44 in destroying multitudes they rushed

---

[1] See chapter 2 of the prophet Joel, where this fine simile of a destroying army is also found.

45 against me.   The dust of their feet like a mighty cloud

46 as they drew nigh to me, the face of heaven

47 darkened before me.   In the city of Khaluli[1]

48 which is on the bank of the Tigris they drew out their battle array—

49 The front of my fenced camp they seized, and discharged their arrows.

50 Then I to Ashur, the Moon, the Sun, Bel, Nebo, Nergal,

51 Ishtar of Niniveh, and Ishtar of Arbela, the gods my protectors

52 that I might conquer my powerful enemies I prayed unto them.

53 My earnest prayers they heard, and came

54 to my assistance.   From my heart I vowed a thank-offering for it.

55 . . . .

56 . . . . . . In my great War Chariot

57 (named) " Sweeper away of enemies," in the fury of my heart

58 I drove rapidly : my great Bow

59 which Ashur gave me, in my hand I took :

60 with greaves of showy workmanship I enclosed my legs;

61 and rushing on the whole army of those wicked enemies

62 in crowded confusion I crushed them together, and like the god Im[2] I thundered.

63 By command of Ashur the great lord, my lord, both to my side and front

---

[1] This account of the battle of Khaluli is the most elaborate that has yet been found in the Assyrian annals.

[2] Im was the god of the sky.   He wielded the thunderbolt, like the Jupiter Tonans of the Latins.

64 as it were fiery darts[1] against my enemies I hurled.

65 In the arms of Ashur my lord, and the shock of my battle

66 furious, I . . . . . .

67 . . . . . The hostile troops with the revolving blades[2]

68 I overthrew: their dead bodies I rolled over

69 in the mire.   Khumban-undash an *engineer*

70 whom the king of Elam had made general of his army,

71 (*had*) his liberation for a great ransom.   His chief officers,

72 who wore gold handled daggers, and with rings

73 *heavy* of bright gold encircled their legs,

74 like a herd of sleek oxen of abundant fatness

75 eagerly I attacked and defeated them.

76 Their heads I cut off, like victims,

77 their highly worked decorations I tore off with derision.

78 Like the fall of a great shower, their rings and bracelets

79 I cast down upon the earth in a lofty heap.

80 My faultless horses yoked to my chariot

81 through the deep pools of blood stepped slowly.

82 Of my chariot, as it swept away the slain and the fallen,

83 with blood and flesh its wheels were clogged.

84 The heads of their soldiers, like *urkiti*

85 I salted, and into great wicker baskets I stuffed them.[3]

---

[1] Frequently spoken of.   Some composition like Greek fire was employed in war.

[2] His chariot wheels were armed with iron scythes—so I understand the passage—See 2 Maccabees xiii. 2, and Xenophon's Anabasis.

[3] To be sent to Nineveh, doubtless, and there exposed on the walls as trophies of his victory.

COLUMN VI.

Line 1 . . . .

2 The bracelets I cut off from their hands

3 The rings *heavy* of gold, of beautiful workmanship, I took off from their feet

4 . . . .

5 the gold and silver handled daggers from their girdles I took.

6 The rest of the Chiefs, and Nebo-zikir-iskun

7 son of Merodach-Baladan who from my battle

8 had fled, but had rallied their forces, alive

9 in the battle my hands seized them. The chariots

10 and horses, whose drivers in the great battle

11 had been killed, ...

12 ran away by themselves, in multitudes.

13 I returned when the fourth hour of the night was past,

14 and stopped the slaughter. He himself, Umman-Minan

15 king of Elam, and the kings of Babylon, and the princes

16 of Chaldæa who had come with him, by the tumult of my battle

17 were overwhelmed: they abandoned their tents

18 and to save their lives, the dead bodies of their own soldiers they trampled underfoot

19 and fled *like frightened birds* who had lost all heart.

20 In double numbers they crowded into their chariots,

21 set off, and fled away to their own dominions.

22 My chariots and horses I despatched after them,

23 and those fugitives who fled for their lives

24 wherever they came up with them, they put them to the sword.

---

25 In the course of those days, after that the Central palace of Niniveh

26 for my royal residence I had finished,

27 and had filled it with beauties to the admiration of mankind,

28 (I turned to) the Kurili palace, which for the lodging of a garrison,

26 the care of horses, and for other needs of every kind

30 the kings my fathers, who went before me, had made—

31 Its mound had never been finished; of its small building

32 the fabric had never been repaired : for a long time

33 its *timin* had been lost : its foundations were laid bare : its summits had fallen down.

34 That palace I pulled down the whole of it.

35 A great quantity of earth from the low lying fields

36 and outskirts of the city, in baskets I took, and upon it

37 I added what was left of the ruins of the former palace :

38 then with the earth of the low grounds which I took from the river side,

39 I completed the mound. Two hundred fathoms

40 altogether, I extended its wall. In a prosperous month

41 and on a lucky day, upon that mound, with the skilfulness of my mind

42 a Palace of stone and cedar wood in the building style

43 of the land of Syria, and a Palace of the lofty architecture of Assyria

44 which beyond the former one was much finer, larger,

45 and more beautiful, in the year of the Eponymy of my great bow bearer

46 the master of my arms, for my royal dwelling I began to build.

47 Long beams of cedar wood, the growth of the land of Khamanu

48 and its lofty mountains, I laid as a roof over them.

49 doors of *liari* wood, inlaid with shining brass

50 I framed, and I fitted them to the gates—

51 Of the white stone which in the district

52 of Balada is found, great bulls and lions

53 I made, and I placed them right and left

54 of the gates.   For the reception of royal guests[1] *(I destined it),* and also for the care

55 of horses, *mules, cattle, flocks,*

56 chariots, *wine presses to make wine,*

57 bows and arrows, and every kind of implement of war,

58 harnesss of horses and *mules*

59 which had great strength, and were trained to the yoke.

60 The courts of the building I enlarged greatly—

61 That palace from its foundations to its summit

62 I built and finished.   The written records of my name

63 I placed within it.   In future days,

64 under the kings my sons, whom Ashur and Ishtar

65 unto the sovereignty of this land and people shall call

66 their names ; when this Palace shall grow old

67 and decay, the future King who shall repair its injuries,

68 who shall see the written records of my name,

69 who shall build an altar, sacrifice a male victim, and replace it in its place,

70 Ashur and Ishtar will receive his prayers—

[1] In fact, another inscription (R. 44, 68), says that all the kings of Phœnicia came there *at the same time.*

71 The destroyer of my writings and my name

72 may Ashur, the great lord, the father of the gods, deliver him to his enemies,

73 his sceptre and his throne take away from him, and destroy his life !

---

74 In the month of Adar, day the twentieth, in the eponymy of Bel-silal-ani

75 prefect of Karkamish.

THE

ANNALS OF ASSURBANIPAL,

THE SARDANAPALUS OF THE GREEKS.

By GEORGE SMITH.

CYLINDER A.

THE text of Cylinder A of Assurbanipal is compiled from a terra cotta cylinder found by Mr. Loftus in the North Palace, Kouyunjik, and the fragments of several duplicate cylinders from the same place. All these inscriptions are now in the British Museum.

A copy of this text was published in the Cuneiform Inscriptions of Western Asia, Vol. iii. p. 17-26.

Translations of parts of the Egyptian campaigns were published by Sir H. C. Rawlinson, in the " *Transactions of the Royal Society of Literature,*" Vol. vii. 137; and by M. Oppert, in his " *Mémoire sur les rapports de l'Egypte et l'Assyrie, dans l'antiquité éclairés par l'étude des texts Cunéiformes;"*[1] and the complete text of the Cylinder, accompanied by an ·interlinear transcription and translation, was published by Mr. G. Smith in his "*History of Assurbanipal.*"

[1] Accompanied by parts of the texts.

TRANSLATION OF THE INSCRIPTION.

COLUMN I.

1 I AM Assurbanipal, the progeny of Assur and Beltis,

2 son of the great king of Riduti,[1]

3 whom Assur and Sin the lord of crowns, from days remote,

4 prophesying his name, have raised to the kingdom,

5 and in the womb of his mother, have created him to rule Assyria.

6 Shamas, Vul, and Ishtar, in their supreme power,

7 commanded the making of his kingdom.

8 Esarhaddon, king of Assyria, the father my begetter,

9 the will of Assur and Beltis the gods his protectors praised,

10 who commanded him to make my kingdom.

11 In the month Iyyar the month of Hea, lord of mankind,

12 on the 12th day, a fortunate day, the festival of Bel;

13 in performance of the important message which Assur,

14 Beltis, Sin, Shamas, Vul, Bel, Nebo,

15 Ishtar of Nineveh, Sarrat-Kitmuri,[2]

16 Ishtar of Arbela, Ninip, Nergal, and Nusku had spoken,

17 he gathered the people of Assyria, small and great,

---

[1] Riduti is the name of the north palace Kouyunjik.

[2] Kitmuri was a temple at Nineveh.

18 and of the upper and lower sea ;

19 to the consecration of my royal sonship,

20 and afterwards the kingdom of Assyria I ruled.

21 The worship of the great gods I caused to be offered to them,

22 I confirmed the covenants.

23 With joy and shouting

24 I entered into Riduti the palace,

25 the royal property of Sennacherib, the grandfather my begetter,

26 the son of the great king, who ruled the kingdom within it,

27 the place where Esarhaddon, the father my begetter,

28 within it grew up, and ruled the dominion of Assyria.

29 . . . . . . and the family increased

30 . . . .

31 I Assurbanipal within it, preserved

32 the wisdom of Nebo, all the royal tablets,

33 the whole of the clay tablets, all there were, their subjects I studied.

34 I collected arrows, bows, carriages, horses,

35 chariots, their furniture and fittings. By the will of the great gods

36 who . . . . . . I proclaimed their laws,

37 they commanded the making of my kingdom,

38 the embellishing of their temples they entrusted to me,

39 for me they exalted my dominion, and destroyed my enemies.

40 The man of war, the delight of Assur and Ishtar,

41 the royal offspring am I.

42 When Assur, Sin, Shamas, Vul, Bel, Nebo, Ishtar of Nineveh,

43 Sarrat-Kitmuri, Ishtar of Arbela, Ninip, Nergal, and Nusku

44 firmly seated me on the throne of the father my begetter,

45 Vul poured down his rain, Hea feasted his people,

46 fivefold[1] the seed bore in its ear,

47 the surplus grain was two-thirds, the crops were excellent,

48 the corn abundant, my face *was pleased* with the raising of the harvest,

49 . . . . . . the cattle were good in multiplying,

50 in my seasons there was plenty, in my years famine was ended.

---

51 In my first expedition to Makan[2]

52 and Milukha[3] I went. Tirhakah king of Egypt and Ethiopia,

53 of whom, Esarhaddon king of Assyria, the father my begetter, his overthrow had accomplished ;

54 and had taken possession of his country ; he Tirhakah,

55 the power of Assur, Ishtar, and the great gods my lords

56 despised, and trusted to his own might.

57 Of the kings and governors, whom in the midst of Egypt,

58 the father my begetter had appointed; to slay, plunder,

59 and to capture Egypt, he came against them ;

60 he entered, and sat in Memphis, the

61 city which the father my begetter had taken, and to the boundaries

62 of Assyria had added. I was going in state in the midst of Nineveh,

---

[1] Variant reading : fourfold.   [2] Makan supposed to be Egypt.
[3] Milukha supposed to be Meroe.

63 and one came and repeated *this* to me ;

64 over these things

65 my heart was bitter and much afflicted ;

66 *by the command* of Assur and the goddess Assuritu,

67 I gathered my powerful forces,

68 which Assur and Ishtar had placed in my hands,

69 to Egypt and Ethiopia I directed the march.

70 In the course of my expedition, 22 kings

71 of the side of the *sea and the middle of the sea,* all

72 tributaries dependent *on me,*

73 to my presence *came and kissed my feet.*

74 Those kings . . . . . .

75 on sea and land *their roads I took,*

76 the level path . . . . . .

77 for the restoration of the kings and governors

78 who in the midst of Egypt *were* tributaries dependent
on me ;

79 quickly I descended and went to Karbanit.

80 Tirhakah king of Egypt and Ethiopia, in the midst
of Memphis,

81 of the progress of my expedition heard ; and to
make war,

82 fighting and battle, to my presence he gathered the
men of his army.

83 In the service of Assur, Ishtar, and the great gods,
my lords,

84 on the wide battle field I accomplished the overthrow
of his army.

85 Tirhakah in the midst of Memphis, heard of the
defeat of his army ;

86 the terror of Assur and Ishtar overcame him, and

87 he went forward; fear of my kingdom

88 overwhelmed him, and his gods glorified me before
my camp.

89 Memphis he abandoned, and to save his life
90 he fled into Thebes. That city I took,
91 my army I caused to enter, and rest in the midst
of it.
92 Necho[1] king of Memphis and Sais.
93 Sarludari king of Pelusium.
94 Pisan-hor king of Natho.
95 Paqruru king of Pi-supt.[2]
96 Pukkunanni-hapi king of Athribis.
97 Nech-ke king of Henins.
98 Petubastes king of Tanis.
99 Unamunu king of Natho.
100 Horsiesis king of Sebennytus.
101 Buaiuva king of Mendes.
102 Sheshonk king of Busiris.
103 Tnephachthus king of Bunubu.[3]
104 Pukkunanni-hapi king of Akhni.
105 Iptikhardesu king of Pizatti-hurunpiku.
106 Necht-hor-ansini king of Pi-sabdinut.
107 Bukur-ninip king of Pachnut.
108 Zikha king of Siyout.
109 Lamintu king of Chemmis.
110 Ispimathu king of Abydos.
111 Munti-mi-anche king of Thebes.
112 These kings, prefects, and governors,
113 whom in the midst of Egypt, the father my begetter
had appointed;
114 who before the advance of Tirhakah
115 their appointments had left, and fled to the desert,
116 I restored; and the places of their appointments

[1] Necho was father of Psammitichus I.
[2] Mentioned in the stele of Mt. Barkal.
[3] See Penub the modern Badnub in the "*Inscription of Pianchi*," by Canon Cook, p. 17.

117 in their possessions, I appointed them.

118 Egypt and Ethiopia, which the father my begetter had captured,

119 again I took, the bonds more than in former days

120 I strengthened, and I made covenants.

121 With abundant plunder and much spoil

122 in peace I returned to Nineveh.

123 Afterwards all those kings whom I had appointed,

124 sinned against me ; they did not keep the oath of the great gods,

(*Continued on Column* II.)

COLUMN II.

1 the good I did to them they despised,

2 and their hearts devised evil;

3 seditious words they spoke, and

4 evil council they counselled among themselves;

5 thus: "Tirhakah from the midst of Egypt

6 is cut off, and to us our seats are numbered."

7 Unto Tirhakah king of Ethiopia

8 to make agreement and alliance

9 they directed their messengers,

10 thus: "May an alliance by this treaty be established, and

11 we will help each other;

12 the country on the other side we will strengthen, and

13 may there not be in this treaty any other lord."

14 Against the army of Assyria the force of my dominion,

15 which to their aid had been raised, they devised

16 a wicked plot. My generals of this plot

17 heard; their messengers

18 and their dispatches they captured, and saw

19 their seditious work. These kings

20 they took; and in bonds of iron and fetters of iron,

21 bound their hands and feet. The oath of Assur king of the gods

22 took them who sinned

23 against the great (gods); who had sought the good of their hands, and

24 who had given them favours;

25 and the people of Sais, Mendes, Zoan,

26 *and* the rest of the cities, all with them *revolted*

27 devised an evil design. Small and great with the sword they caused to be destroyed

28 one they did not leave in the midst.

29 Their corpses they threw down in the dust,

30 . . . . . . they destroyed the towers of the cities.

31 These kings, who had devised evil

33 against the army of Assyria, alive to Nineveh

33 into my presence they brought.

34 To Necho . . . . . . of them,

35 favour I granted him, and a covenant . . . .

36 Observances stronger than before I caused to be restored, and with him I sent.

37 Costly garments I placed upon him, ornaments of gold,

38 his royal image I made for him, rings of gold I fastened on his feet,

39 a steel sword its sheath of gold,

40 in the glory of my name more than I write I gave him.

41 Chariots, horses, and mules

42 for his kingdom I appointed ;

43 my generals as governors,

44 to *Egypt* with him I sent.

45 The place where the father my begetter, in Sais to the kingdom had appointed him,

46 to his district I restored him ;

47 (and) Neboshazban his son in Athribes.

48 Benefits and favours, beyond *those* of the father my begetter,

49 I caused to restore, and gave to him.

50 Tirhakah to *Ethiopia* fled ;

51 the might of the soldiers of Assur my lord overwhelmed him, and

52 he went to his place of night.[1]

53 Afterwards Rudammon, son of his sister,

54 sat on his royal throne.

55 Thebes his fortified city he made, and

56 he gathered his forces

[1] *I. e.* he died.

57 to fight my army, *the sons* of Assyria ;

58 who within Memphis gathered in the midst of *it.*

59 . . . . and besieged and took the whole of them.

60 . . . . came and told me.

---

61 In my second expedition, to Egypt and Ethiopia

62 I directed the march. Rudammon of

63 the progress of my expedition heard, and that I had crossed over

64 the borders of Egypt. Memphis he abandoned, and

65 to save his life he fled into Thebes.

66 The kings, prefects, and governors, whom in Egypt I had set up,

67 to my presence came, and kissed my feet.

68 After Rudammon the road I took ;

69 I went to Thebes, the strong city ;

70 the approach of my powerful army he saw, and Thebes he abandoned,

71 and fled to Kipkip. That city[1]

72 the whole of it, in the service of Assur and Ishtar my hands took ;

73 silver, gold, precious stones, the furniture of his palace, all there was ;

74 garments costly and beautiful, great horses,

75 people male and female,

76 two lofty obelisks covered with beautiful carving,

77 . . hundred talents their weight, set up before the gate of a temple,

78 with them I removed, and brought to Assyria.

79 *Its spoils* unnumbered I carried off.   From the midst of Thebes,

80 over Egypt and Ethiopia ;

[1] Thebes.

6

81 my servants I caused to march, and

82 I acquired glory. With the tributes

83 peacefully I returned to Nineveh, the city of my dominion.

---

84 *In my third expedition* against Bahal king of Tyre

85 . . . I went; who my royal will

86 disregarded, and did not hear the words of my lips;

87 towers round him I raised;

88 on sea and land; his roads I took;

89 their spirits I humbled and caused to melt away;

90 to my yoke I made them submissive. The

91 daughter proceeding from his body, and the daughters of his brothers

92 for concubines he brought to my presence.

93 Yahimelek *his* son, the glory of the country, of unsurpassed renown

94 at once he sent forward, to make obeisance to me.

95 His daughter and the daughters of his brothers,

96 with their great dowries I received.

97 Favour I granted him, and the son proceeding from his body

98 I restored and gave him. Yakinlu

99 king of Arvad, dwelling in the midst of the sea,

100 who to the kings my fathers was not submissive,

101 submitted to my yoke, his daughter

102 with many gifts, for a concubine

103 to Nineveh he brought, and kissed my feet.

104 Mugallu king of Tubal, who against the kings my fathers

105 made attacks, the daughter proceeding from his body,

106 and her great dowry, for a concubine

107 to Nineveh he brought, and kissed my feet.
108 Over Mugallu great horses
109 an annual tribute I fixed upon him.
110 Sandasarmi of Cilicia,
111 who to the kings my fathers did not submit,
112 and did not perform their pleasure,
113 the daughter proceeding from his body, with many
114 gifts, for a concubine
115 to Nineveh he brought, and kissed my feet.
116 When Yakinlu king of Arvad,
117 had met his death.   Azibahal, Abibahal,
118 Adonibahal, Sapadibahal, Pudibahal,
119 Bahalyasup, Bahalhanun,
120 Bahalmaluk, Abimelek, and Ahimelek,
121 sons of Yakinlu, dwelling in the midst
122 of the sea, from the midst of the sea arose, and
123 with their numerous presents
124 came and kissed my feet.
125 Azibahal gladly I received, and
126 to the kingdom of Arvad appointed.
127 Abibahal, Adonibahal, Sapadibahal,

(*Continued on Column* III.)

COLUMN III.

1 Pudibahal, Bahalyasup, Bahalhanon,

2 Bahalmelek, Abimelek, and Ahimelek ;

3 costly clothing . . . . rings . . . . . .

4 in my presence . . . . .

5 Gyges king of Lydia,

6 a district which is across the sea, a remote place,

7 of which the kings my fathers had not heard speak of its name ;

8 the account of my grand kingdom in a dream was related to him by Assur, the god my creator,

9 thus : " The yoke . . . .

10 (when) in remembrance . . . . . .

11 the day *he saw that* dream,

12 his messenger *he sent, to pray for my friendship.*

13 that dream *which he saw,*

14 by the hand of his envoy he sent, and repeated *to me.*

15 From the midst of the day when he took the yoke of *my kingdom,*

16 the Cimmerians, wasters of *his* people,

18 who did not fear my fathers

18 and me, and did not take the yoke of my kingdom, he captured,

19 in the service of Assur and Ishtar the gods my lords.

20 From the midst of the chiefs of the Cimmerians, whom he had taken,

21 two chiefs in strong fetters of iron, and bonds of iron,

22 he bound, and with numerous presents,

23 he caused to bring to my presence.

24 His messengers whom, to pray for my friendship

25 he was constantly sending, he wilfully discontinued

26 as the will of Assur, the god my creator, he had disregarded ;

27 to his own power he trusted and hardened his heart.

28 His forces to the aid of Psammitichus (king) of Egypt,

29 who had thrown off the yoke of my dominion, he sent; and

30 I heard *of it*, and prayed to Assur and Ishtar

31 Thus : " Before his enemies his corpse may they cast, and

32 may they carry captive his attendants." When thus to Assur

33 I had prayed, he requited me. Before his enemies his corpse

34 was thrown down, and they carried captive his attendants.

35 The Cimmerians whom by the glory of my name he had trodden under him ;

36 conquered and swept the whole of his country after him his son

37 sat on his throne, that evil work at the lifting up of my hands,

38 the gods my protectors in the time of the father his begetter had destroyed.

39 By the hand of his envoy he sent and took the

40 yoke of my kingdom thus : " The king whom God has blessed art thou ;

41 my father from *thee* departed, and evil was done in his time ;

42 I am thy devoted servant, and my people all perform thy pleasure."

---

43 In my fourth expedition, I gathered my army ;

44 against Akhseri king of Minni[1]

[1] Minni bordered on Armenia.

45 I directed the march.

46 By command of Assur, Sin, Shamas, Vul, Bel, Nebo,

47 Ishtar of Nineveh, Sarrat-Kitmuri,

48 Ishtar of Arbela, Ninip, Nergal, Nusku ;

49 into Minni I entered, and marched victoriously ;

50 his strong cities and smaller ones, which were without number,

51 to the midst of Izirtu, I took ;

52 I threw down, destroyed, and in the fire I burned. People, horses,

53 asses, oxen, and sheep, from the midst of those

54 cities I brought out, and as a spoil I counted.

55 Ahseri of the progress of my expedition heard ; and

56 abandoned Izirtu his royal city ;

57 to Istatti his castle he fled, and

58 took refuge.   That district I took ;

59 for fifteen days' journey[1] I laid waste, and

60 the highlands I conquered.

61 Ahseri, not fearing my power,

62 by the will of Ishtar dwelling in Arbela, who from the first had spoken

63 thus : "I am the destroyer of Ahseri, king of Minni."

64 When I had commanded it, it was accomplished. Into the hands of his

65 servants she delivered him, and the people of his country a revolt against him made, and

66 in front of his city his attendants threw down and

67 tore in pieces his corpse.   His brothers, his relatives,

68 and the seed of the house of his father, they destroyed with the sword.

69 Afterwards Vaalli his son sat on his throne ;

70 the power of Assur, Sin, Shamas, Vul, Bel, Nebo,

---

[1] A day's journey was about fourteen or fifteen miles.

71 Ishtar of Nineveh, Sarrat-Kitmuri,

72 Ishtar of Arbela, Ninip, Nergal, and Nusku,

73 the great gods my lords, he saw, and submitted to my yoke.

74 To preserve his life his hand he opened and besought

75 my power. Erisinni, his eldest son,

76 to Nineveh he sent, and kissed my feet.

77 Favour I granted him, and my messenger for friendship

78 I sent to him. The daughter proceeding from his body

79 he sent for a concubine.

80 The former tribute, which in the time of the kings my fathers

81 they had broken off, he had brought to my presence.

82 Thirty horses, beside the former tribute, I added and fixed upon him.

---

83 In my fifth expedition, to Elam I directed the

84 march. By the command of Assur, Sin, Shamas, Vul, Bel, Nebo,

85 Ishtar of Nineveh, Sarrat-Kitmuri,

86 Ishtar of Arbela, Ninip, Nergal and Nusku ;

87 in the month Elul, the month of the king of the gods, Assur,

88 the father of the gods, the glorious prince : like the shock of a terrible storm,

89 I overwhelmed Elam, through its extent.

90 I cut off the head of Teumman, their wicked king ;

91 who devised evil. Beyond number I slew his soldiers ;

92 alive in hand, I captured his fighting men.

93 Their wives, like bows and arrows,

94 filled the vicinity of Shushan.

95 Their corpses the Ulai,[1] I caused to take,

[1] The Ulai is the river mentioned in Daniel.

96 its waters I made to consume like chaff.

97 Ummanigas son of Urtaki, king of Elam,

98 who from the face of Teumman to Assyria

99 fled, and had taken my yoke ;

100 with me I brought him to Elam.

101 I seated him on the throne of Teumman.

102 Tammarit his third brother, who with him

103 fled ; in Hidalu I appointed to the kingdom.

104 Then the servants of Assur and Ishtar, over Elam

105 I caused to march ; I acquired power

106 and glory.   On my return

107 against Dunanu the Gambulian,[1] who to Elam

108 trusted ; I set my face.   Sapibel

109 the fortified city of Gambuli, I took ;

110 into that city I entered, its people entirely

111 I carried off.   Dunanu and Samgunu,

112 opposers of the work of my kingdom,

113 in strong fetters of iron, and bonds of iron,

114 I bound their hands and feet.   The rest of the sons
of Belbasa,

115 his kin, the seed of his father's house, all there were,

116 Nabonidus and Beledir, sons of Nebozikiresses

117 the tigenna, and the attendants of the father their
begetter ;

(*Continued on Column* IV.)

---

[1] Gambuli was in the marshes south of Babylonia.

COLUMN IV.

1 with the . . . . . and Tebe,

2 people of Gambuli, oxen, sheep, asses,

3 horses, and mules ; from the midst of Gambuli,

4 *I carried off* to Assyria. Sapibel, his

5 fortified city, *I pulled down*, destroyed, and into the waters I turned.

---

6 . . . . . . Saulmugina my younger *brother ; benefits I had given* to him, and

7 *had appointed him to the kingdom of* Babylon . . . . . and gave him

8 . . . . . chariots I fixed, and

9 . . . . . . cities, fields and plantations.

10 *Tribute* and taxes, I caused to return, and more than the father my begetter,

11 *I did for him.* And he these favours

12 *disregarded*, and devised evil.

13 *The yoke of my dominion*, he threw off, the benefits

14 . . . . . . strengthener of men

15 . . . . . . over Assyria I ruled.

16 *To pray for* my *friendship* ceased, and

17 enemies in ships . . . with them,

18 pretending to pray for my friendship ;

19 to Nineveh, to *my presence* he sent them.

20 I am Assurbanipal king of Assyria, *to whom* the great gods' excellent fame have

21 renowned him. His might in . . . and dominion.

22 The sons of Babylon of them *in* state chairs

23 I set them up ; costly garments

24 I placed upon them, rings of gold I fastened on

25 their feet, and the sons of Babylon of them

26 in Assyria they were set up, they were honoured

27 before the giving of my command.   And he Saul-mugina

28 my younger brother; who did not keep my agreement,

29 the people of Akkad, Chaldea, Aram, and the sea coast,

30 from Aqaba to Babsalimitu,

31 tributaries dependent on me; he caused to revolt against my hand.

32 And Ummanigas the fugitive, who took

33 the yoke of my kingdom, of whom in Elam,

34 I had appointed him to the kingdom; and the kings of Goim,

35 Syria and Ethiopia,

36 which, by command of Assur and Beltis, my hands held;

37 all of them against me he caused to rebel, and

38 with him they set their faces.   The people of Sippara,

39 Babylon, Borsippa, and *Kutha*, broke off the brother-hood,

40 and the walls of those cities his fighting men he

41 Caused to raise; with me they made war,

42 making . . . . my, from the face of Bel son of Bel,

43 the light of the gods Shamas, the warrior Ninip, he revolted; and

44 he caused to cease . . . . gift of my fingers,

45 to capture the cities, seats of the gods, of whom their temples

46 I had restored, adorned with gold and silver,

47 and within them had fixed images; he devised evil.

48 In those days, then a seer in the beginning of the night, slept and

49 dreamed a dream, thus: "Concerning the matter which Sin was arranging, and

50 of them who against Assurbanipal king of Assyria,

51 devised evil. Battle is prepared; a—

52 violent death I appoint for them. With the edge of the sword,

53 the burning of fire, famine, and the judgment of Ninip, I will destroy

54 their lives." This I heard, and trusted to the will of Sin

55 my lord. In my sixth expedition I gathered my army;

56 against Saulmugina I directed the march.

57 Within Sippara, Babylon, Borsippa, and Kutha,

58 him and part of his fighting men I besieged, and captured

59 the whole of them in town and country, without number.

60 I accomplished his overthrow. The rest,

61 in the judgment of Ninip, drought and famine

62 passed their lives. Ummanigas king of Elam,

63 appointed by my hand; who the bribe received, and came to his aid.

64 Tammaritu against him revolted, and him

65 and part of his family he destroyed with the sword.

66 Afterwards Tammaritu, who after Ummanigas,

67 sat on the throne of Elam,

68 did not seek alliance with my kingdom. To the help of

69 Saulmugina my rebellious brother,[1] he went and

70 to fight my army, he prepared his soldiers.

71 In prayer to Assur and Ishtar, I prayed;

72 my supplications they received,[2] and heard the words of my lips.

73 Indabigas his servant, against him revolted, and

74 in the battlefield accomplished his overthrow. Tammaritu king of Elam,

[1] Variant: younger brother.   [2] Variant: took.

75 who over the decapitated head of Teumman untruth
had spoken ;

76 which he had cut off in the sight of my army,

77 thus : " I have *not* cut off the head of the king of
Elam

78 . . . . in the assembly of his army."   Again he said :

79 "And Ummanigas only, kissed the ground ;

80 in the presence of the envoys of Assurbanipal king of
Assyria."

81 For these matters, which he had mocked,

82 Assur and Ishtar turned from him ; and Tammaritu

83 his brothers, his kin, the seed of his father's house
with eighty-five princes

84 going before him from the face of Indabigas

85 fled, and their bitterness within their hearts

86 raged, and they came to Nineveh.

87 Tammaritu my royal feet kissed, and

88 earth he threw on his hair, standing at my footstool

89 *He* to do my service himself set,

90 for the giving of his sentence, and going to his help.

91 By the command of Assur and Ishtar, he submitted
to my dominion.

92 In my presence he stood up, and glorified the

93 might of my powerful gods, who went to my help.

94 I Assurbanipal, of generous heart,

95 of defection the remover, forgiver of sin ;

96 to Tammaritu favour I granted him, and

97 himself, and part of the seed of his father's house
within my palace,

98 I placed them.   In those days the people of Akkad,

99 who with Saulmugina were placed,

100 and devised evil ; famine took them,

101 for their food the flesh of their sons and their
daughters,

102 they did eat, and divided the . . . . .

103 Assur, Sin, Shamas, Vul, Bel, Nebo,

104 Ishtar of Nineveh, the divine queen of Kitmuri,

105 Ishtar of Arbela, Ninip, Nergal and Nusku,

106 who in my presence marched and destroyed my enemies :

107 Saulmugina my rebellious brother,

108 who made war with me ; in the fierce burning fire

109 they threw him, and destroyed his life.

110 And the people who to Saulmugina

111 my rebellious brother, he had caused to join,

112 and these evil things did ;

113 who death deserved, their lives

114 before them being precious :

115 with Saulmugina their lord,

116 they did not burn in the fire, before the edge of the sword,

117 dearth, famine, and the burning fire, they had fled, and

118 taken refuge.   The stroke of the great gods

119 my lords, which was not removed

120 overwhelmed them.   One did not flee,

121 a sinner did not escape from my hands,

122 my hands held *them*.   Powerful war chariots,

123 covered chariots, his concubines *and*

(*Continued on Column* V.)

COLUMN V.

1 the goods¹ of his palace, they brought *to* my presence.

2 Those men *who* the curses of their mouth,

3 against Assur my god curses uttered ;

4 *and against* me, the prince his worshipper, had devised evil :

5 their tongues I pulled out, their overthrow I accomplished.

6 The rest of the people alive among the stone lions and bulls,

7 which Sennacherib the grandfather my begetter, in the midst had thrown ;

8 again I in that pit, those men

9 in the midst threw.   The limbs cut off

10 I caused to be eaten by dogs, bears, eagles,

11 vultures, birds of heaven, and fishes of the deep.

12 By these things *which* were done,

13 I satisfied the hearts of the great gods my lords.

14 The bodies of the men whom Ninip had destroyed,

15 and who in drought and famine had passed their lives ;

16 . . . . dogs, bears,

17 saturi, burru . . . . grew fat.

18 Their attendants from the midst of Babylon,

19 Kutha and Sippara, I brought out

20 and placed in slavery.

21 In splendour, the seats of their sanctuaries I built.

22 I raised their glorious towers.

23 Their gods dishonoured, their goddesses desecrated

24 I rested in purple and hangings.

25 Their institutions, which they had removed, like in days of old,

¹ Variant: furniture.

26 in peace I restored and settled.

27 The rest of the sons of Babylon, Kutha,

28 and Sippara, who under chastisement, suffering,

29 and privation had fled ;

30 favour I granted them, the saving of their lives I commanded :

31 in Babylon I seated them.

32 The people of Akkad, and some of Chaldea, Aram and

33 the sea ; whom Saulmugina had gathered,

34 . . returned to their own districts.

35 They revolted against me. By command of Assur and Beltis

36 and the great gods my protectors, on the whole of them I trampled,

37 the yoke of Assur which they had thrown off, I fixed on them ;

38 prefects and rulers appointed by my hand,

39 I established over them.

40 The institutions and high ordinances of Assur and Beltis,

41 and the gods of Assyria, I fixed upon them ;

42 taxes and tribute to my dominion,

43 of the country the sum undiminished I fixed on them.

---

44 In my seventh expedition, in the month Sivan the month of Sin lord of might,

45 eldest son and first of Bel : I gathered my army,

46 against Ummanaldas[1] king of Elam I directed

47 the march. I brought with me Tammaritu king of Elam,

48 who from the face of Indabigas his servant had fled, and

49 taken my yoke. The people of Hilmi, Billati,

50 Dummuqu, Sulai, Lahira and Dibirina,

[1] Ummanaldas was son of Attamitu, commander of the archers ; he murdered and succeeded Indabigas.

51 the force of my fierce attack, heard of, as I went to Elam.

52 the terror of Assur and Ishtar my lords, and the fear of my kingdom

53 overwhelmed them.   They, their people, their oxen and their sheep,

54 to do my service to Assyria they struck, and

55 took the yoke of my kingdom.   Bitimbi the former

56 royal city, the fortress of Elam ;

57 which like a wall the boundary of Elam divided,

58 which Sennacherib king of Assyria, the grandfather my begetter,

59 my predecessor, had captured : and he the Elamite,

60 a city in front of the former Bitimbi,

61 another had built, and its wall he had strengthened, and

62 had raised its outer wall Bitimbi

63 he had proclaimed its name : in the course of my expedition I took.

64 The people dwelling in it, who did not come out, and did not pray for

65 alliance with my kingdom, I felled.   Their heads I cut off, their lips

66 I tore out, and for the inspection of the people of my country, I brought to Assyria.

67 Imbaappi governer[1] of Bitimbi,

68 the relative of Ummanaldas king of Elam ;

69 alive from the midst of that city

70 I brought out and hand and foot in bonds of iron I placed him, and

71 sent to Assyria.   The women of the palace, and sons

72 of Teumman king of Elam ; whom by the command of Assur,

[1] Variant: commander of the archers.

73 In my former expedition I had cut off his head ;

74 with the rest of the people dwelling in Bitimbi,

75 I brought out and as spoil I counted. Ummanaldas king of Elam,

76 *of the progress of* my *army*, which into Elam entered ; heard, and

77 Madaktu his royal city he abandoned, and fled and his mountains ascended.

78 Umbagua[1] who from Elam, from a revolt,

79 to Bubilu had fled, and against Ummanaldas

80 had sat on the throne of Elam : like him also heard, and

81 Bubilu the city the seat of his dominion he abandoned, and

82 like the fishes took to the depths of the remote waters.

83 Tammaritu who fled and took my yoke,

84 into Shushan I caused to enter, I appointed him to the kingdom.

85 The good I had done to him and sent to his aid, he rejected and

86 devised evil to capture my army.

87 Even he said in his heart thus : " The people of Elam

88 for a spoil have turned, in the face of Assyria.

89 Their . . . has been entered and they have carried away

90 the plunder of Elam." Assur and Ishtar who before me[2] march,

91 and exalt me over my enemies ;

92 the heart of Tammaritu hard and perverse they broke, and

93 took hold of his hand, from the throne of his kingdom

94 they hurled him, and overwhelmed him, a second time

95 they subdued him to my yoke.

96 concerning these matters, in vexation was my heart ;

[1] Variant : Ambagua.　　　　[2] Variant : in my presence.

7

97 which Tammaritu the younger offended.

98 In the glory and power of the great gods my lords,

99 within Elam, through its extent I marched victoriously.

100 On my return, peace and submission

101 to my yoke, I restored to Assyria.

102 Gatudu, Gatuduma, Daeba,

103 Nadiha, Duramnani, Duramnanima,

104 Hamanu, Taraqu, Haiusi,

105 Bittagilbitsu, Bitarrabi,

106 Bitimbi Madaktu, Shushan,

107 Bube, Temaruduksaranni,

108 Urdalika, Algariga,

109 Tubu, Tultubu,

110 Dunsar, Durundasi, Durundasima,

111 Bubilu, Samunu, Bunaki,

112 Qabrina, Qabrinama and Haraba,

113 their cities I captured, pulled down, destroyed,

114 in the fire I burned ; their gods, their people,

115 their oxen, their sheep, their furniture, their goods,

116 carriages, horses, mules,

117 and weapons, instruments of war, I carried off to Assyria.

---

118 In my eighth expedition, by command of Assur and Ishtar,

119 I gathered my army, against Ummanaldas

120 king of Elam I directed the march.

121 Bitimbi, which in my former expedition

122 I had captured, again Rasi, Hamanu,

123 and that district I captured ; and he Ummanaldas

124 king of Elam, of the capture of Rasi and Hamanu

125 heard, and fear of Assur and Ishtar going before me—

(*Continued on Column* VI.)

COLUMN VI.

1 overwhelmed him, and Madaktu his royal city
2 he abandoned, and fled to Durundasi.
3 The Itite, he crossed, and that river
4 for his stronghold he fixed,
5 and arranged in ranks to fight me.
6 Naditu the royal city and its district I captured,
7 Bitbunaki the royal city ditto,
8 Hardapanu the royal city ditto,
9 Tubu the royal city ditto,
10 beside all the river, Madaktu the royal city ditto,
11 Haltemas his royal city I captured,
12 Shushan his royal city I captured,
13 Dinsar, Sumuntunas ditto,
14 Pidilma his royal city, Bubilu ditto,
15 Kabinak *his royal city* ditto.
16 In the service of Assur and Ishtar I marched and
went
17 after Ummanaldas king of Elam,
18 who did not submit to my yoke. In the course of
my expedition,
19 Durundasi his royal city I captured.
20 My army the Itite in high flood
21 saw, and feared the crossing.
22 Ishtar dwelling in Arbela, in the middle of the night
to my army
23 a dream sent, and even told them,
24 thus : "I march in front of Assurbanipal, the king
25 whom my hands made." Over that vision
26 my army rejoiced, and the Itite crossed peacefully.
27 Fourteen cities royal seats, and smaller cities
28 the numbers unknown, and twelve districts

29 which are in Elam, all of them I took,

30 I pulled down, destroyed, in the fire I burned, and to mounds and heaps I reduced.

31 Without number I slew his warriors,

32 with the sword I destroyed his powerful fighting men.

33 Ummanaldas king of Elam

34 in his bitterness fled, and took to the mountain.

35 Banunu and the districts of Tasara

36 all, twenty cities in the districts

37 of Hunnir, by the boundary of Hidalu, I captured.

38 Balimmu and the cities round it,

39 I pulled down and destroyed. Of the people dwelling within them,

40 their misfortune I caused, I broke up their gods,

41 I set at liberty the great goddess of the lord of lords,

42 his gods, his goddesses, his furniture, his goods, people small and great,

43 I carried off to Assyria. Sixty kaspu[1] of ground,

44 by the will of Assur and Ishtar who sent me,

45 within Elam I entered and marched victoriously.

46 On my return, when Assur and Ishtar exalted me

47 over my enemies, Shushan the great city,

48 the seat of their gods, the place of their oracle, I captured.

49 By the will of Assur and Ishtar, into its palaces I entered

50 and sat with rejoicing. I opened also their treasure houses,

51 of silver, gold, furniture and goods, treasured within them ;

52 which the kings of Elam the former,

53 and the kings who were to these days,

54 had gathered and made ; which any other enemy

---

[1] A kaspu was about seven miles.

55 beside me, his hands had not put into them,

56 I brought out and as a spoil I counted.

57 Silver, gold, furniture and goods, of Sumir Akkad

58 and Gandunias, all that the kings of

59 Elam, the former and *latter*, had carried off

60 and brought within Elam ; bronze hammered,

61 hard, and pure, precious stones beautiful and valuable,

62 belonging to royalty; which kings of Akkad former ones

63 and Saulmugina, for their aid had paid

64 to Elam : garments beautiful, belonging to royalty,

65 weapons of war, prepared for one to make battle,

66 suited to his hand, instruments furnishing his palaces,

67 all that within it was placed, with the food

68 in the midst *which* he ate and drank, and the couch he reclined on,

69 powerful war chariots,

70 of which their ornaments were bronze and paint,

71 horses and great mules,

72 of which their trappings were gold and silver, I carried off to Assyria.

73 The tower of Shushan which in the lower part in marble was laid,

74 I destroyed. I broke through its top, which was covered with shining bronze.

75 Susinaq the god of their oracle, who dwelt in the groves ;

76 whom any one had not seen the image of his divinity,

77 Sumudu, Lagomer, Partıkira,

78 Ammankasibar, Uduran and Sapak ;

79 of whom the kings of Elam worship their divinity.

80 Ragiba, Sumugursara, Karsa,

81 Kirsamas, Sudunu, Aipaksina,

82 Bilala, Panintimri, Silagara,

83 Napsa, Nabirtu and Kindakarbu,

84 these gods and goddesses, with their valuables,

85 their goods, their furniture, and priests, and

86 worshippers, I carried off to Assyria.

87 Thirty-two statues of kings, fashioned of silver, gold, bronze

88 and alabaster, from out of Shushan,

89 Madaktu and Huradi,

90 and a statue of Ummanigas son of Umbadara,

91 a statue of Istarnanhundi, a statue of Halludus

92 and a statue of Tammaritu the later,

93 who by command of Assur and Ishtar made submission to me,

94 I brought to Assyria.   I broke the winged lions

95 and bulls watching over the temple, all there were.

96 I removed the winged bulls attached to the gates of

97 the temples of Elam, until they were not, I overturned.

98 His gods and his goddesses I sent into captivity,

99 their forest groves,

100 which any other had not penetrated into the midst,

101 had not trodden their outskirts ;

102 my men of war into them entered,

103 saw their groves, and burned *them* in the fire.

104 The high places of their kings, former and latter,

105 not fearing Assur and Ishtar my lords,

106 opposers of the kings my fathers,

107 I pulled down, destroyed and burnt in the sun.

108 their attendants I brought to Assyria,

109 their leaders without shelter I placed.

110 The wells of drinking water I dried them up,

111 for a journey of a month and twenty-five days the districts of Elam I laid waste,

112 destruction, servitude and drought I poured over them.

113 The daughters of kings, consorts of kings,

114 and families former and latter

115 of the kings of Elam, the governors and

116 citizens of those cities,

117 all I had captured; the commanders of archers, prefects,

118 directors of . . , three horse charioteers

119 chariot drivers, archers, officers,

120 camp followers and the whole of the army, all there was,

121 people male and female, small and great, horses,

122 mules, asses, oxen and sheep,

123 beside much spoil, I carried off to Assyria.

COLUMN VII.

1 The dust of Shushan, Madaktu,

2 Haltemas, and the rest of their cities,

6 entirely I brought to Assyria.

4 For a month and a day, Elam to its utmost extent I swept ;

5 the passage of men, the treading of oxen and sheep,

6 and the springing up of good trees I burnt off the fields.

7 Wild asses, serpents beasts of the desert and ugalhus,

8 safely I caused to lay down in them.

9 Nana, who 1,635 years[1]

10 had been desecrated, had gone, and dwelt

11 in Elam, a place not appointed to her ;

12 and in those days, she and the gods her fathers,

13 proclaimed my name to the dominion of the earth.

14 The return of her divinity she entrusted to me,

15 thus: "Assurbanipal, from the midst of Elam (wicked),

16 bring me out, and cause me to enter into Bitanna."

17 The will commanded by their divinity, which from days remote

18 they had uttered ; again they spoke to later people.

19 The hands of her great divinity I took hold of, (and)

20 the straight road rejoicing in heart,

21 she took to Bitanna.

22 In the month Kislev, the first day, into Erech I caused her to enter, and

23 In Bithilianni which she had delighted in,

24 I set her up an enduring sanctuary.

[1] The image of the goddess Nana was carried away by Kudur-nanhundi, king of Elam.

25 People and spoil of Elam,

26 which by command of Assur, Sin, Shamas, Vul, Bel, Nebo,

27 Ishtar of Nineveh, the divine queen of Kitmuri,

28 Ishtar of Arbela, Ninip, Nergal and Nusku, I had carried away ;

29 the first part to my gods I devoted.

30 The archers, footmen,

31 soldiers and camp followers

32 whom I carried off from the midst of Elam ;

33 over the body of my kingdom I spread.

34 The rest to the cities seats of my gods,

35 my prefects, my great men, and all my camp,

36 like sheep I caused to overflow.

37 Ummanaldas king of Elam,

38 who the vigour of the powerful soldiers of Assur and Ishtar had seen ;

39 from the mountain, the place of his refuge, he returned and

40 into Madaktu, the city which by command of Assur and Ishtar

41 I had pulled down, destroyed and carried off its spoil ;

42 he entered and sat in sorrow, in a place dishonoured.

43 Concerning Nebobelzikri, the grandson of Merodach-baladan ;

44 who against my agreement had sinned, and thrown off the yoke of my dominion :

45 who on the kings of Elam to strengthen him had relied,

46 had trusted to Ummanigas, Tammaritu,

47 Indabigas, and Ummanaldas,

48 kings who had ruled the dominion of Elam.

49 My envoy about the surrender of Nebobelzikri,

50 with determination of purpose I sent

51 to Ummanaldas.　Nebobelzikri, grandson of Mero-
dachbaladan,

52 of the journey of my envoy who into Elam had entered

53 heard, and his heart was afflicted.　He inclined to
despair,

54 his life before him he did not regard, and

55 longed for death ;

56 to his own armour-bearer he said also

57 thus : " Slay me with the sword."

58 He and his armour-bearer with the steel swords of
their girdles pierced through

59 each other.　Ummanaldas feared, and the

60 corpse of that Nebobelzikri *who* benefits trampled on,

61 with the head of his armour-bearer who destroyed
him with the sword,

62 to my envoy he gave, and he sent it to my presence.

63 His corpse I would not give to burial

64 more than before his death I returned, and

65 his head I cut off ; round the neck of Neboqatizabat

66 the munmakir of Saulmugina

67 my rebellious brother, who with him to pass into

68 Elam had gone ; I hung.

69 Pahe who against Ummanaldas,

70 had ruled the dominion of Elam,

71 the terror of the powerful soldiers of Assur and
Ishtar,

72 who the first, second, and third time had trampled
over Elam

73 covered him, and he trusted to the goodness of my
heart,

74 from the midst of Elam he fled and

75 took the yoke of my kingdom.

76 The people, sinners of Bitimbi,

77 Kuzurtein, Dursar,

78 Masutu, Bube.

79 Bitunzai, Bitarrabi.

80 Iprat, Zagar of Tapapa,

81 Akbarina, Gurukirra,

82 Dunnushamas, Hamanu,

83 Kanizu, Aranzese,

84 Nakidati, Timinut of Simami,

85 Bitqatatti, Sakisai,

86 Zubahe, and Tulhunba,

87 who in my former expedition, from the face of the powerful soldiers

88 of Assur and Ishtar fled and

89 took to Saladri, a rugged mountain ;

90 those people who on Saladri

91 the mountain fixed their stronghold,

92 the terror of Assur and Ishtar my lords overwhelmed them ;

93 from the mountain the place of their refuge they fled and

94 took my yoke ; to the bow I appointed them,

95 over the body of my kingdom

96 which filled my hand I spread.

---

97 In my ninth expedition I gathered my army,

98 against Vaiteh king of Arabia

99 I directed the march, who against my agreement

100 had sinned ; the benefits done to him he did not regard, and

101 threw off the yoke of my dominion.

102 When Assur had set him up to perform my pleasure,

103 to seek my alliance his feet broke off, and

104 he ended his presents and great tribute.

105 When Elam was speaking sedition with Akkad, he heard and

106 disregarded my agreement.   Of me Assurbanipal,

107 the king, the noble priest, the powerful leader,

108 the work of the hands of Assur, he left me, and

109 to Abiyateh and Aimu, sons of Tehari,

110 his forces with them to the help of

111 Saulmugina my rebellious brother he sent, and

112 set his face.   The people of Arabia

113 with him he caused to revolt, and carried away the

114 plunder of the people whom Assur, Ishtar, and the great gods

115 had given me, their government I had ruled,

116 and they were in my hand.

117 By command of Assur and Ishtar my army in the region of

118 Azaran, Hirataqaza,

119 in Edom, in the neighbourhood of Yabrud,

120 in Beth Ammon, in the district of the Hauran,

121 in Moab, in Saharri,

122 in Harge, in the district of Zobah.

COLUMN VIII.

1 His numerous fighting men I slew without number, I accomplished

2 his overthrow. The people of Arabia, all who with him came,

3 I destroyed with the sword ; and he from the face of the

4 powerful soldiers of Assur, fled and got away

5 to a distance. The tents, the pavilions,

6 their dwellings, a fire they raised, and burned in the flames.

7 Vaiteh, misfortune happened to him, and

8 alone he fled to Nabatea.

9 Vaiteh son of Hazael, brother of the father

10 of Vaiteh son of Birvul, whom the people of his country

11 appointed to the kingdom of Arabia ;

12 Assur king of the gods the strong mountain, a decree

13 repeated, and he came to my presence.

14 To satisfy the law of Assur and the great gods

15 my lords, a heavy judgment took him, and

16 in chains I placed him, and with asi and dogs

17 I bound him, and caused him to be kept in the

18 great gate in the midst of Nineveh Nirib-barnakti-adnati

19 and he Ammuladi[1] king of Kedar,

20 brought to fight the kings of Syria,

21 whom Assur and Ishtar the great gods had entrusted to me.

22 In the service of Assur, Sin, Shamas, Vul, Bel, Nebo,

23 Ishtar of Nineveh Sarrat-Kitmuri,

[1] Ammuladi was captured by the king of Moab, who sent him to Assyria.

24 Ishtar of Arbela, Ninip, Nergal and Nusku,

25 his overthrow I accomplished.   Himself alive with *Adiya*

26 the wife of Vaiteh king of Arabia,

27 they captured and brought to my presence.

28 By command of the great gods my lords, with the dogs

29 I placed him, and I caused him to be kept chained.

30 By command of Assur, Ishtar, and the great gods my lords,

31 of Abiyateh and Aimu sons of Tehari,

32 who to the help of Saulmugina my rebellious brother

33 to enter Babylon went;

34 his helpers I slew, his overthrow I accomplished. The remainder

35 who into Babylon entered, in want and

36 hunger ate the flesh of each other.

37 To save their lives, from the midst of Babylon

38 they came out, and my forces which around Saulmugina

39 were placed, a second time his overthrow accomplished ; and

40 he alone fled, and to save his life

41 took my yoke.   Favour I granted him and

42 an agreement to worship the great gods I caused him to swear, and

43 instead of Vaiteh or anyone,

44 to the kingdom of Arabia I appointed.

45 And he with the Nabateans

46 his face set, and the worship of the great gods did not fear, and

47 carried away the plunder of the border of my country.

48 In the service of Assur, Sin, Shamas, Vul, Bel, Nebo,

49 Ishtar of Nineveh Sarrat-Kitmuri,

50 Ishtar of Arbela, Ninip, Nergal and Nusku,

51 Nathan king of Nabatea, whose place was remote,
52 of whom Vaiteh to his presence (had) fled ;
53 heard also of the power of Assur who protected me :
54 who in time past to the kings my fathers,
55 his envoy did not send, and did not seek
56 alliance with their kingdom ; in fear of the soldiers of
Assur
57 capturing . . . . he tore and sought alliance
58 with my kingdom. Abiyateh
59 son of Teheri did not . . . benefits, disregarding the
60 oath of the great gods, seditious words against me
61 he spoke, and his face with Nathan
62 king of Nabatea he set ; and their forces
63 they gathered to commit evil against my border.
64 By command of Assur, Sin, Shamas, Vul, Bel, Nebo,
65 Ishtar of Nineveh Sarrat-Kitmuri,
66 Ishtar of Arbela, Ninip, Nergal and Nusku,
67 my army I gathered ; against Abiyateh
68 I directed the march. The Tigris
69 and the Euphrates in their flood (strong) peacefully
they crossed,
70 they marched, a distant path they took, they ascended
71 the lofty country they passed through the forests,
72 of which their shadow was vast, bounded by trees
great and strong,
73 and vines a road of mighty wood.
74 They went to the rebels of Vas, a place arid and
75 very difficult, where the bird of heaven had not . . . . .
76 wild asses they found not in it.
77 100 kaspu of ground, from Nineveh
78 the city the delight of Ishtar, wife of Bel ;
79 against[1] Vaiteh king of Arabia
80 and Abiyateh with the forces

[1] Variant: after.

81 of the Nabateans, they went.

82 They marched and went in the month Sivan, the month of Sin

83 the eldest son and first of Bel,

84 the twenty-seventh day, on the festival of the lady of Babylon,

85 the mighty one of the great gods.

86 From Hadatta I departed ;

87 in Laribda a tower of stones,

88 over against lakes of water ; I pitched my camp.

89 My army the waters for their drink desired, and

90 they marched and went over arid ground, a place very difficult,

91 to Hurarina near Yarki,

92 and Aialla in Vas, a place remote,

93 a place the beast of the desert was not in,

94 and a bird of heaven had not fixed a nest.

95 The overthrow of the Isammih, the servants

96 of Adarsamain, and the Nabateans

97 I accomplished.   People, asses, camels,

98 and sheep, their plunder innumerable ; I carried away.

99 Eight kaspu of ground my army

100 marched victoriously, peacefully they returned, and

101 in Aialli they drank abundant waters ;

102 from the midst of Aialli to Quraziti.

103 six kaspu of ground, a place arid and very difficult,

104 they marched and went. The worshippers of Adarsamain,

105 and the Kidri of Vaiteh,

106 son of Birvul¹king of Arabia, I besieged ;

107 his gods, his mother, his sister, his wife, his kin,

108 the people in the midst all, the asses,

¹ Variant: Birdadda.

109 camels, and sheep ;

110 all in the service of Assur and Ishtar my lords

111 my hands took. The road to Damascus

112 I caused their feet to take. In the month Ab, the month of Sagittarius

113 daughter of Sin the archer; the third day, the festival

114 of the king of the gods, Merodach, from Damascus

115 I departed. Six kaspu of ground in their country all of it.

116 I marched, and went to Hulhuliti.

117 In Hukkuruna, the rugged mountain,

118 the servants of Abiyateh son of Tehari of

119 Kedar I captured ; his overthrow I accomplished,

120 I carried off his spoil. Abiyateh and Aimu,

121 sons of Tehari, by command of Assur and Ishtar my lords,

122 in the midst of battle alive I captured in hand.

123 Hand and foot in bonds of iron I placed them,

(*Continued on Column* IX.)

8

COLUMN IX.

1 with the spoil of their country I brought them

2 to Assyria.   The fugitives, who from the face of my soldiers

3 fled, ascended and took to

4 Hukkuruna the rugged mountain.

5 In Laanhabbi . . . . .

6 . . . . .

Lines 7 to 25 are lost, only the following ends of eight lines remain :—

a . . .	*e* . . strong
b . . . and	*f* . . camels
c . . .	*g* . . . .
d . . them	*h* . . . .

26 oxen, sheep, asses, camels

27 and men, they carried off without number.

28 The sweeping of all the country through its extent,

29 they collected through the whole of it.

30 Camels like sheep I distributed and

31 caused to overflow to the people of Assyria

32 dwelling in my country.   A camel

33 for half a shekel, in half shekels of silver, they valued in front of the gate ;

34 the spoil in the sale of captives among the strong

35 . . . . . . which were gathered in droves,

36 they bartered camels and men.

37 Vaiteh and the Arabians,

38 who my agreement . . . . . .

39 who from the face of the soldiers of Assur *my* lord,

40 fled and got away ;

41 Ninip the warrior destroyed,

42 in want *and famine their lives* were spent, and

43 for their food they eat the flesh of their children.

44 With a curse . . . . . . mud of the earth

45 in the house of Assur father of *the gods* . . . them

46 Assur, Sin, Shamas, Vul, Bel, Nebo,

47 Ishtar of Nineveh, Sarrat-Kitmuri,

48 Ishtar of Arbela, Ninip, Nergal, Nusku,

49 camels strong, oxen and sheep,

50 more than seven the sacrificers sacrificed, and

51 for eating they did not eat their carcases.

52 The people of Arabia one to another, addressed each other

53 thus : " Concerning the number of these

54 evil things which happened to Arabia,

55 because the great agreements with Assur we have not regarded ;

56 and we have sinned against the benefits of Assur-banipal,

57 the king, the delight of the heart of Bel."

58 Beltis the consort of Bel,

59 the guardian of divinity ;

60 who with Anu and Bel in dominion

61 is established : pierced my enemies with horns of iron.

62 Ishtar dwelling in Arbela, with fire clothed ;

63 . . . . drought upon Arabia poured down.

64 Dabara the warrior, mourning caused and

65 destroyed my enemies.

66 Ninip fierce, the great warrior,

67 the son of Bel ; with his mighty arrows

68 destroyed the life of my enemies.

69 Nusku the glorious messenger, sitting in dominion ;

70 who by command of Assur and Beltis . . . .

71 The archer, the goddess of . . . . .

72 my forces preceded, and . . . . . . place of my kingdom,

73 the front of my army took and

74 destroyed my enemies.

75 The stroke . . . Assur, Ishtar,

76 and the great gods my lords,

77 who in making *war*, went to the help of

78 my army : Vaiteh heard of, and

79 over *these things* feared, and

80 from *Nabatea I* brought out, and

81 in the service of Assur, Sin, Shamas, Vul, Bel, Nebo,

82 Ishtar of Nineveh Sarrat-Kitmuri,

83 Ishtar of Arbela, Ninip, Nergal and Nusku,

84 . . . . him, and sent him to Assyria.

85 . . . . . who to capture my enemies

86 . . . fought.   By command of Assur and Beltis

87 with a mace which was grasped by my hand,

88 the flesh coming out of him, his son,

89 in sight of his eyes I struck down.

90 With the dogs I did not place him,

91 in the gate of the rising sun, in the midst of Nineveh,

92 which Nirib-parnakti-adnati[1] is called its name ;

93 I caused to keep him chained,

94 to exalt the will of Assur Ishtar and the great gods

95 my lords.   Favour I granted him, and saved his life.

96 On my return Hosah,

97 which by the side of the sea has its place, I captured.

98 The people of Hosah, who to their prefects

99 were not reverent, and did not give the tribute,

100 the gift of their country, I slew.   Amongst the people

101 unsubmissive, chastisement I inflicted.

102 Their gods and their people I carried off to Assyria.

[1] The name of the eastern gate of Nineveh.

103 The people of Akko unsubmissive I destroyed.

104 Their bodies in the dust I threw down ; the whole of the city

105 I quieted.   The rest of them I brought

106 to Assyria, in rank I arranged, and

107 over my numerous army,

108 which Assur strengthened, I spread.

109 Aimu son of Tehari, with Abiyateh

110 his brother had risen, and with my army had made war.

111 In the midst of battle, alive in hand I captured ;

112 in Nineveh the city of my dominion his skin I tore off.

113 Ummanaldas king of Elam,

114 whom from of old Assur and Ishtar my lords

115 had commanded to make submission to me ;

116 by command of their great divinity who were unchanged,

117 afterwards his country against him revolted, and

118 from the face of the tumult of his servants which they made against him,

119 alone he fled and took to the mountain.

120 From the mountain, the house of his refuge,

121 the place he fled to,

122 like a raven I caught, and

(*Continued on Column* X.)

COLUMN X.

1 alive I brought him to Assyria.

2 Tammaritu, Pahe and Ummanaldas,

3 who after each other ruled the dominion of Elam ;

4 whom, by the power of Assur and Ishtar my lords,

5 I subjugated *to* my *yoke.* Vaiteh

6 king of Arabia, of whom, by command of Assur and Ishtar, his overthrow

7 I had accomplished ; *from* his country I brought him *to* Assyria.

8 When to . . . sacrifices and libations I had offered up

9 in Masmasu, the seat of their power,

10 before Beltis, mother of the great gods,

11 beloved wife of Assur, I had made to the gods of

12 Idkid. To the yoke of my war chariot

13 I caused to fasten them, and to the gate of the temple

14 they drew it. On my feet I made invocation,

15 I glorified their divinity, I praised

16 their power, in the assembly of my army ; of Assur, Sin,

17 Shamas, Vul, Bel, Nebo, Ishtar of Nineveh

18 Sarrat-Kitmuri, Ishtar of Arbela,

19 Ninip, Nergal and Nusku, who the unsubmissive to me,

20 subjugated to my yoke, and in glory

21 and power established me over my enemies.

---

22 Saduri, king of Ararat ; who the kings his fathers

23 to my fathers had sent in fellowship.

24 Again, Saduri, the mighty things

25 for which the great gods had caused renown to me, heard, and

26 like a son to his father, he sent to my dominion ;
27 and he in these words sent
28 thus : " Salutation to the king my lord."
29 Reverently and submissively his numerous presents
30 he sent to my presence.

---

31 Now Riduti, the private palace of Nineveh,
32 the grand city, the delight of Ishtar ;
33 which Sennacherib king of Assyria, the grandfather my begetter
34 built for his royal seat ;
35 that Riduti in my days
36 became old, and its chamber-walls decayed.
37 I, Assurbanipal, the great king, the powerful king,
38 king of nations, king of Assyria, king of the four regions,
39 within that Riduti grew up.
40 Assur, Sin, Shamas, Vul, Bel, Nebo, Ishtar of Nineveh Sarrat-Kitmuri,
41 Ishtar of Arbela, Ninip, Nergal and Nusku,
42 my royal sonship . . . .
43 . . . their good protection,
44 . . . . over me
45 *fixed*, when on the throne of the father my begetter I sat.
46 They were made (?) . . . . and many people
47 . . . . my hands
48 . . . . . . me within it.
49 On my couch at night . . . . my
50 in . . . .
51 that mastaku . . . .
52 the great gods its renown have heard . . . good,
53 its decay . . . to enlarge it

54 . . . . the whole of it I destroyed.

55 . . . Fifty tipki the building its sculpture

56 . . . . the work of the mound I completed.

57 Before the temples of the great gods my lords

58 I worshipped. . . . Of that mound

59 its sculpture I did not cut down its top.

60 In a good month and a prosperous day, upon that mound its

61 foundation I placed, I fixed its brickwork.

62 In biris and kamis its face I . . . .

63 I divided in three . . .

64 in chariots of Elam,

65 which by command of the great gods my lords

66 I carried off; to make that Bitriduti,

67 the people of my country in the midst, took its bricks.

68 The kings of Arabia who against my agreement sinned

69 whom in the midst of battle alive I had captured *in hand*,

70 to make that Bitriduti

71 heavy burdens *I caused them to carry, and*

72 I caused them to take . . . .

73 building its brickwork . . . .

74 with dancing and music . . . .

75 with joy and shouting, from *its foundation to its roof*

76 I built. More than before . . . . . .

77 I extended . . . .

78 beams and great planks from Sirara

79 and Lebanon, I fixed over it.

80 Doors of forest trees, their wood excellent,

81 a covering of copper I spread over, and hung in its gates.

82 Great columns of bronze . . . .

83 at the sides of the gates . . . . .

84 That Riduti, my royal seat,

85 the whole of it I finished, entirely

86 I completed. Plantations choice,

87 . . . . for the glory of

88 my kingdom I planted like walls.

89 Sacrifices and libations precious I poured out to the gods my lords.

90 With joy and shouting I completed it,

91 I entered into it in a state palanquin.

92 I after days, among the kings my sons,

93 whomever Assur and Ishtar to the dominion of the country and people

94 shall proclaim his name ;

95 when this Riduti becomes old and

96 decays, its decay he shall repair,

97 the inscription written of my name my father's and my grandfather's,

98 the remote descendant who . . . . may he see, and

99 an altar may he raise, sacrifice and libations may he pour out,

100 and with the inscription written of his name may he place ;

101 may the great gods all in this inscription named,

102 like me also, establish to him

103 power and glory.

104 Whoever the inscription written of my name,

105 my father's and my grandfather's, shall destroy,

106 and with his inscription shall not place,

107 Assur, Sin, Shamas, Vul, Bel, Nabu,

108 Ishtar of Nineveh, Sarrat-Kitmuri,

109 Ishtar of Arbela, Ninip, Nergal and Nusku,

110 a judgment equal to the renown of my name, may they pass on him.

111 Month Nisan, 1st day,
112 eponym[1] Shamasdainani prefect of Akkad.

DATE ON ANOTHER COPY.

a Month Elul, 28th day,
b eponym Shamasdainani prefect of Babylon.

[1] The eponyms were annual officers, after whom the years were named.

INSCRIPTION OF DARIUS

ON THE ROCK

AT BEHISTUN.

TRANSLATED BY

SIR H. RAWLINSON, K.C.B., D.C.L., ETC.

THE great triumphal tablet of Darius Hystaspes, exhibiting the figures of the victorious king and his attendants and of ten vanquished Chiefs, and accompanied by a record in three languages, which extends to nearly a thousand lines of Cuneiform writing, is engraved on the face of a precipitous rock at Behistun[1] near the town of Kermanshah on the Western frontiers of Media.

The inaccessibility of the Sculptures, which are at the height of at least 400 feet above the plain, had deterred all the early Persian travellers from attempting to copy the Inscriptions. At length however Major Rawlinson, who was employed on military duty in the province, succeeded

[1] το Βαγίστανον ὄρος of the Greek; *i.e. Baz-istan* or " Place of the God."

in scaling the rock in the autumn of 1835; and between
that period and the close of 1837 when his services were
transferred to Teheran, having repeatedly visited the spot,
he contrived to make a copy of a considerable portion of
the Arian version of the record.   During the two following
years he was busily employed in decyphering and translat-
ing the portion which he had thus copied, and his various
letters on the subject were read before the Royal Asiatic
Society on January 4, 1840, as reported in the *Athenæum*,
No. 639, p. 79.   An interval of inaction now occurred, as
Major Rawlinson was summoned to take part in the Afghan
war; but in 1843 he returned to Baghdad, and in the sum-
mer of the following year he once more visited Behistun;
and on this occasion as he was furnished with ladders,
he completed his copy of the Arian text, and also recovered
considerable portions both of the Scythic and Semitic
versions.

The long expected Memoir on the Arian or Persian text
of the great Behistun Inscription was completed in 1845,
and was published in the *Journal of the Royal Asiatic
Society* for 1846.   There were still however some passages in the Arian text which required verification and
completion, while of the other versions — especially of
the Semitic version, the value of which as a key to the

decypherment of the independent Inscriptions of Assyria and Babylonia was becoming daily more apparent—large portions were entirely uncopied, so that one more visit to the Behistun rock was deemed indispensable. This was accordingly accomplished in 1848, when Major Rawlinson not only obtained a large list of emendations and restorations of the published Arian text, but also carried off his most valuable trophy in a complete set of paper casts of the entire Scythic and Semitic versions, so far as the writing could be at all distinguished on the rock.

In the following year Major Rawlinson returned to England and published the latest results of his labours, the corrections of the Persian text appearing in the *Journal of the Royal Asiatic Society* under date Feb. 1, 1850, and the Semitic text being given at length with an analysis in the 14th volume of the Journal early in the ensuing year.

On returning to Baghdad at the close of 1851, Major Rawlinson handed over his casts of the Scythic version to Mr. E. Norris, the well known Oriental scholar, who published from them an independent translation of the great Behistun Inscription in the *Journal of the Royal Asiatic Society* for 1852.

The translation which here follows is based upon Major Rawlinson's original reading of the Arian text as published in 1846, but it also includes his emendations of 1850, and is further strengthened by additions from Mr. Norris's Scythic Memoir of 1852, while in a few instances advantage has been taken of Monsieur Jules Oppert's matured dissection of the Semitic version published in 1858, to give greater completeness to the record.

The translation given by Professor Rawlinson in his *Herodotus* Vol. ii. p. 590, has also been compared, and German criticism has occasionally furnished an improved reading.

TRANSLATION OF THE INSCRIPTION.

COLUMN I.

Paragraph 1 I am Darius, the great King, the King of Kings, the King of Persia, the King of the provinces, the son Hystaspes, the grandson of Arsames, the Achæmenian.

2 Says Darius the King:—My father was Hystaspes; of Hystaspes the father was Arsames; of Arsames the father was Ariyaramnes; of Ariyaramnes the father was Teispes; of Teispes the father was Achæmenes.

3 Says Darius the King:—On that account we are called Achæmenians; from antiquity we have descended; from antiquity those of our race have been kings.

4 Says Darius the King:—There are eight of my race who have been kings before me, I am the ninth; for a very long time[1] we have been kings.

5 Says Darius the King:—By the grace of Ormazd I am king; Ormazd has granted me the empire.

6 Says Darius the King:—These are the countries which belong to me—by the grace of Ormazd I have become king of them—Persia, Susiana, Babylonia, Assyria, Arabia, Egypt, those which are of the sea,[2] Sparta, Ionia, Media, Armenia, Cappadocia, Parthia, Zarangia, Aria, Chorasmia, Bactria, Sogdiana, Gandara, the Sacæ, the Sattagydes, Arachosia, and Mecia, in all twenty-three countries.

7 Says Darius the King:—These are the countries which belong to me; by the grace of Ormazd they have become subject to me—they have brought tribute to me. That which has been said unto them by me, both by night and by day it has been performed by them.

---

[1] Or, in a double line.   [2] *I.e.*, the Islands of the Mediterranean.

Paragraph 8 says Darius the King :—Within these countries whoever was good, him have I cherished and protected ; whoever was evil, him have I utterly destroyed. By the grace of Ormazd these countries have obeyed my laws.   As to them it has been said by me, thus has it been done by them.

9 Says Darius the King :—Ormazd granted me the empire.   Ormazd brought help to me so that I gained this empire.   By the grace of Ormazd I hold this empire.

10 Says Darius the King :—This (is) what was done by me, before I became king. He who was named Cambyses[1] the son of Cyrus of our race, he was here king before me. There was of that Cambyses a brother named Bardes ; he was of the same father and mother as Cambyses. Afterwards Cambyses slew this Bardes.   When Cambyses slew Bardes it was not known to the state that Bardes was killed. Then Cambyses proceeded to Egypt.   When Cambyses had gone to Egypt, the state became wicked ; then the lie became abounding in the land, both in Persia and in Media, and in the other provinces.

11 Says Darius the King:—Afterwards there was a certain man, a Magian, named Gomátes. He arose from Pissiachádá, the mountain named Arakadres, from thence ; on the 14th day of the month Viyakhana[2] then it was that he arose.   To the state he thus falsely declared : " I am Bardes the son of Cyrus, the brother of Cambyses."   Then the whole state became rebellious ; from Cambyses it went over to him, both Persia and Media, and the other provinces. He seized the empire ; on the 9th day of the month Garmapada,[3] then it was he thus seized the empire.   Afterwards Cambyses, killing himself died.

12 Says Darius the King:—The empire, of which Gomátes, the Magian, dispossessed Cambyses, that empire

---

[1] Kabujiya.   [2] The 12th month.   [3] The 5th month.

had been in our family from the olden time.   After Gomátes
the Magian had dispossessed Cambyses of Persia and Media
and the dependent provinces, he acted with his own party (?)
he became king.

13 Says Darius the King :—There was not a man, neither
Persian, nor Median, nor any one of our family, who could
dispossess of the empire that Gomátes, the Magian.   The
state feared him exceedingly.   He slew many people who
had known the old Bardes ; for that reason he slew the
people " Lest they should recognize me that I am not
Bardes the son of Cyrus."   There was not any one bold
enough to say aught against Gomátes the Magian until I
arrived.   Then I prayed to Ormazd ; Ormazd brought help
to me.   On the 10th day of the month Bágayádish[1] then it
was, with my faithful men[2] I slew that Gomátes, the Magian
and the chief men who were his followers.   The fort
named Sictachotes, in the district of Media, named Nisæa,
there I slew him ; I dispossessed him of the empire.   By
the grace of Ormazd I became king ; Ormazd granted me
the sceptre.

14 Says Darius the King :—The empire that had been
wrested from our race, that I recovered, I established it
in its place ; as in the days of old ; thus I did.   The
temples which Gomátes the Magian had destroyed, I rebuilt ; I reinstituted for the state the sacred chaunts and
(sacrificial) worship, and confided them to the families which
Gomátes the Magian had deprived of those offices.   I
established the kingdom in its place, both Persia and Media,
and the other provinces ; as in the days of old ; thus I
restored that which had been taken away.   By the grace of
Ormazd I did this.   I laboured until I had established our
family in its place as in the days of old.   I laboured, by the

---

[1] The 1st month.   [2] Or with a few men.

grace of Ormazd, (in order) that Gomátes the Magian might not supersede our family.

15 Says Darius the King :—This is that which I did after that I became king.

16 Says Darius the King :—When I had slain Gomátes the Magian, then a certain man, named Atrines, the son of Opadarmes, he arose ; to the state of Susiana he thus said : " I am King of Susiana." Then the people of Susiana became rebellious ; they went over to that Atrines ; he became King of Susiana. And a certain man, a Babylonian, named Nadinta-belus the son of Ænares, he arose. The state of Babylonia he thus falsely addressed : "I am Nabochodrossor, the son of Nabonidus." Then the entire Babylonian state went over to that Nadinta-belus. Babylon became rebellious. He seized the government of Babylonia.

17 Says Darius the King :—Then I sent to Susiana; that Atrines was brought to me a prisoner. I slew him.

18 Says Darius the King :—Then I proceeded to Babylon against that Nadinta-belus, who was called Nabochodrossor. The forces of Nadinta-belus held the Tigris ; there they had come, and they had boats. Then I divided my army ; one portion I supplied with camels ; the other I mounted on horses (?) ; Ormazd brought help to me ; by the grace of Ormazd I succeeded in passing the Tigris. Then I entirely defeated the army of that Nadinta-belus. On the 27th day of the month of Atriyátiya[1] then it was that we thus fought.

19 Says Darius the King :—Then I marched against Babylon. When I arrived near Babylon, the city named Zázána, upon the Euphrates, there that Nadinta-belus who was called Nabochodrossor, came with a force before me

---

[1] The 9th month.

offering battle. Then we fought a battle. Ormazd brought help to me ; by the grace of Ormazd, I entirely defeated the force of Nadinta-belus. A part of the army was driven into the water ; the water destroyed them. On the 2nd day of the month Anámaka,' then it was that we thus fought the battle.

' The 10th month.

[End of Column No. I, which extends to ninety-six lines, and the writing of which is generally in good preservation.]

COLUMN II.

Paragraph 1 Says Darius the King:—Then Nadinta-belus with a few horsemen fled to Babylon. Then I proceeded to Babylon ; I both took Babylon and seized that Nadinta-belus. Afterwards I slew that Nadinta-belus at Babylon.

2 Says Darius the King :—Whilst I was at Babylon these are the countries which revolted against me : Persis, Susiana, Media, Assyria, Armenia, Parthia, Margiana, Sattagydia, and Sacia.

3 Says Darius the King :—A certain man named Martes, the son of Sisicres ; a city of Persia, named Cyganaca, there he dwelt ; he rose up ; to the state of Susiana he thus said : "I am Imanes, King of Susiana."

4 Says Darius the King:—When I sent to Susiana then the Susians, fearing from me, seized that Martes ; and the chief of their own men slew him.

5 Says Darius the King :—A certain man named Phraortes, a Median, he rose up ; to the state of Media he thus said : "I am Xathrites, of the race of Cyaxares." Then the Median people, which were at home (?) revolted against me. They went over to that Phraortes ; he became King of Media.

6 Says Darius the King:—The army of Persians and Medes that was with me, that army remained faithful to me.[1] Then I sent forth these troops. Hydarnes by name, a Persian, one of my subjects, him I appointed their leader. I thus addressed them : "Go forth and smite that Median State which does not acknowledge me." Then that Hydarnes marched with his army. When he reached Media, a city of Media named Marusia there he engaged the Medes. He who was leader of the Medes could not at all resist

[1] Or, that (army) was few in number.

him. (?) Ormazd brought help to me; by the grace of Ormazd, the troops of Hydarnes entirely defeated the rebel army. On the 27th day of the month Anámaka[1] then it was that the battle was thus fought by them. Afterwards my forces remained at Kapada, a district of Media, until I myself arrived in Media.

7 Says Darius the King:—Then Dadarses by name, an Armenian, one of my servants, him I sent to Armenia. I thus said to him: "Go forth; the rebel state that does not obey me, smite it." Then Dadarses marched. When he reached Armenia, then the rebels, having collected, came before Dadarses arraying their battle. Zoza by name, a village of Armenia, there they engaged. Ormazd brought help to me; by the grace of Ormazd, my forces entirely defeated that rebel army. On the 8th day of the month, Thurawáhara[2] then it was a battle was thus fought by them.

8 Says Darius the King:—For the second time the rebels, having collected, returned before Dadarses arraying battle. The fort of Armenia named Tigra, there they engaged. Ormazd brought help to me; by the grace of Ormazd, my troops entirely defeated that rebel army. On the 18th day of the month of Thurawáhara[2] then it was that the battle was thus fought by them.[3]

9 Says Darius the King:—For the third time the rebels having assembled, returned before Dadarses arraying battle. A fort of Armenia named Uhyama there they engaged. Ormazd brought help to me; by the grace of Ormazd, my forces entirely defeated the rebel troops. On the 9th day of the month Thaigarchish[4] then it was a battle was thus fought by them. Afterwards Dadarses waited for me there until I reached Media.

[1] The 10th month.   [2] The 2nd month.
[3] Dadarses slew 546 of the rebels and took 520 of them prisoners.
[4] The 3rd month.

10 Says Darius the King:—Then he who was named Vomises, a Persian, one of my servants, him I sent to Armenia.   Thus I said to him : " Go forth, the rebel state which does not acknowledge me, smite it."   Then Vomises marched forth.   When he had reached Armenia, then the rebels, having assembled, came again before Vomises to do battle.   A district of Assyria named Atchidu there they engaged.   Ormazd brought help to me ; by the grace of Ormazd, my forces entirely defeated that rebel army.   On the 15th day of the month Anámaka[1] then it was a battle was thus fought by them.[2]

11 Says Darius the King:—For the second time the rebels having assembled, came before Vomises in battle-array.   The district of Armenia, named Otiára, there they engaged.   Ormazd brought help to me ; by the grace of Ormazd, my forces entirely defeated that rebel army.   In the month Thurawáhara, at the full moon (?), then was a battle fought by them.[3]   Afterwards Vomises remained in Armenia, waiting for me, until I reached Media.

12 Says Darius the King :—Then I departed from Babylon ; I proceeded to Media.   When I reached Media, a city of Media, named Gundrusia, there that Phraortes, who was called King of Media, came with an army before me in battle-array.   Then we joined battle.   Ormazd brought help to me ; by the grace of Ormazd, I entirely defeated the forces of Phraortes.   On the 25th day of the month of Adukana[4] then it was we thus fought the battle.

13 Says Darius the King:—Then that Phraortes, with a few horsemen, fled from thence to the district of Media, named Rhages.   Subsequently I despatched forces in pursuit, by whom Phraortes was taken and brought before me.

[1] The 10th month.   [2] They slew of the enemy 2024.
[3] They slew of the enemy 2045 and took 1559 of them prisoners.
[4] The 4th month.

I cut off both his nose and ears and his tongue, and I scourged him (?). He was held chained at my door; all the kingdom beheld him. Afterwards at Ecbatana, there I crucified him; and the men who were his chief followers at Ecbatana, within the citadel I executed them.

14 Says Darius the King:—A certain man, named Sitratachmes, a Sagartian, he rebelled against me. To the State he thus said: "I am the King of Sagartia. I am of the race of Cyaxares." Then I sent forth an army of Persians and Medians. A man named Tachmaspates, a Median, one of my subjects, him I appointed their leader. Thus I addressed them :—"Go forth, the State which is in revolt, and does not acknowledge me, smite it." Then Tachmaspates marched with his army. He fought a battle with Sitratachmes. Ormazd brought help to me; by the grace of Ormazd, my troops entirely defeated the rebel army, and took Sitratachmes, and brought him before me. Then I cut off his nose and his ears, and I scourged him (?). He was kept chained at my door. All the kingdom beheld him. Afterwards I crucified him at Arbela.

15 Says Darius the King:—This is that (which) was done by me in Media.

16 Says Darius the King:—Parthia and Hyrcania revolted against me; they declared for Phraortes. Hystaspes, who was my father, the Parthian forces rose in rebellion against him. Then Hystaspes with a few troops marched forth. Hyspaostisa, a town of Parthia, there he engaged the rebels. Ormazd brought help, by the grace of Ormazd, Hystaspes entirely defeated the rebel army; on the 22nd day of the month of Viyakhna,[1] then it was the battle was thus fought by them.

[End of Column II., which extends like the preceding to ninety-six lines. The writing is a good deal injured by a fissure in the rock which extends the whole length of the tablet.]

[1] The 12th month.

COLUMN III.

Paragraph 1 Says Darius the King :—Then I sent from Rhages a Persian army to Hystaspes. When that army reached Hystaspes, he marched forth with those troops. The city of Parthia named Patigrapana, there he fought with the rebels. Ormazd brought help to me ; by the grace of Ormazd, Hystaspes entirely defeated that rebel army. On the 1st day of the month Garmapada,[1] then it was the battle was thus fought by them.[2]

2 Says Darius the King :—Then the province submitted to me. This is what was done by me in Parthia.

3 Says Darius the King :—The province named Margiana, that revolted against me. A certain man named Phraates, the Margians made him their leader. Then I sent to him one who was named Dadarses, a Persian, one of my subjects, and the Satrap of Bactria. Thus said I to him : " Go forth ; attack that province which does not acknowledge me." Then Dadarses marched with his forces ; he joined battle with the Margians. Ormazd brought help to me ; by the grace of Ormazd my troops entirely defeated the rebel army. On the 23rd day of the month Atriyátiya[3] then it was the battle was thus fought by them.[4]

4 Says Darius the King :—Then the province submitted to me. This is what was done by me in Bactria.

5 Says Darius the King :—A certain man named Veisdátes ; a city named Tárba, in the district of Persia, named Yutiya, there he dwelt. He rose up a second time ; to the state of Persia he thus said : " I am Bardes, the son of Cyrus." Then the Persian forces, which were at home being removed (?) from connexion with me, (?) they revolted

[1] The 5th month.   [2] He slew of them 6560 and took 4182 prisoners.
[3] The 9th month.
[4] Dadarses slew 4203 of the enemy and took 6562 prisoners.

against me. They went over to that Veisdátes; he became king of Persia.

6 Says Darius the King :—Then I sent forth the Persian and Median forces which were with me. Artabardes by name, one of my servants, him I appointed their chief. Another Persian force accompanied me to Media. Then Artabardes, with his troops, marched to Persia. When he reached Persia, a city of Persia named Racha, there that Veisdátes, who was called Bardes, came with a force against Artabardes to do battle. Then they joined battle. Ormazd brought help to me ; by the grace of Ormazd, my troops entirely defeated the army of Veisdátes. On the 12th day of the month Thurawáhara[1] then it was the battle was thus fought by them.

7 Says Darius the King :—Then that Veisdátes, with a few horsemen fled from thence to Pissiachádá. From that place, with an army, he came back to do battle against Artabardes. The mountain named Parga, there they fought. Ormazd brought help to me ; by the grace of Ormazd, my troops entirely defeated the army of Veisdátes. On the 6th day of the month of Garmapada[2] then it was that the battle was thus fought by them. Both that Veisdátes they took, and also they took the men who were his principal adherents.

8 Says Darius the King :—Then that Veisdátes, and the men who were his chief followers, at a town of Persia named Chadidia, there I impaled them.

9 Says Darius the King :—That Veisdátes, who was called Bardes, he sent troops to Arachotia, against a man named Vibanus, a Persian, one of my servants and Satrap of Arachotia, and he appointed a certain man to be their leader. He thus addressed them : "Go forth; smite

---

[1] The 2nd month.   [2] The 5th month.

Vibánus, and that state which obeys the rule of King
Darius." Then those forces marched which Veisdátes had
sent against Vibánus, to do battle. A fort named Capis-
canes, there they fought an action. Ormazd brought help
to me ; by the grace of Ormazd, my troops entirely defeated the rebel army. On the 13th day of the month
Anámaka[1] then it was the battle was thus fought by them.

10 Says Darius the King :—A second time, the rebels
having assembled, came before Vibánus, to do battle. The
district named Gadytia, there they fought an action. Ormazd brought help to me; by the grace of Ormazd, my
troops entirely defeated the rebel army. On the 7th day
of the month Viyakhna[2] then it was the battle was thus
fought by them.

11 Says Darius the King :—Then that man who was
the leader of those troops which Veisdátes had sent against
Vibánus, that leader with a few horsemen fled away. A
fort of Arachotia, named Arshada, the native place (?) of
Vibánus, he retired to that place. Then Vibánus with his
troops marched in pursuit. There he took him, and slew
the men who were his chief followers.

12 Says Darius the King :—Then the province submitted
to me. This is what was done by me in Arachotia.

13 Says Darius the King :—Whilst I was in Persia
and Media, for the second time the Babylonians revolted
against me. A certain man named Aracus, an Armenian,
the son of Hañditus, he rose up; a district of Babylon
named Dobáña, from thence he arose ; he thus falsely proclaimed : " I am Nabochodrossor, the son of Nabonidus."
Then the Babylonian state revolted against me ; it went
over to that Aracus; he seized on Babylon; he became
King of Babylonia.

---

[1] The 10th month.   [2] The 12th month.

14 Says Darius the King :—Then I sent troops to Babylon. A Median of the name of Intaphres, one of my servants, him I appointed their leader. Thus I addressed them : "Go forth, smite that Babylonian state, which does not acknowledge me." Then Intaphres with his force marched to Babylon. Ormazd brought help to me ; by the grace of Ormazd Intaphres took Babylon. On the 2nd day of the month Markazana¹ then Aracus, who said "I am Nebochodrossor" was seized and brought to me with his principal followers. Then I made a decree that Aracus and his principal followers should be put to death in Babylon.

¹ The 8th month.

[End of Column III., containing ninety-two lines.]

Paragraph 1 Says Darius the King:—This is what was done by me in Babylonia.

2 Says Darius the King:—This is what I have done. Under the favour of Ormazd, have I always acted. As the kings revolted against me, I fought nineteen battles. By the grace of Ormazd, I smote them, and I made nine kings captive. One was named Gomátes, the Magian; he was an impostor: he said, "I am Bardes, the son of Cyrus;" he threw Persia into revolt. One, an impostor, was named Atrines, the Susian: he thus said, "I am the king of Susiana;" he caused Susiana to revolt against me. One was named Nadinta-belus a native of Babylon; he was an impostor: he thus said, "I am Nabochodrossor, the son of Nabonidus;" he caused Babylonia to revolt. One was an impostor named Martes, a Persian: he thus said, "I am Imanes, King of Susiana;" he threw Susiana into rebellion. One was named Phraortes, a Median; he spake lies: he thus said, "I am Xathrites, of the race of Cyaxares;" he persuaded Media to revolt. One was an impostor named Sitratachmes, a native of Sagartia: he thus said, "I am the King of Sagartia, of the race of Cyaxares;" he caused Sagartia to revolt. One was an impostor named Phraates, a Margian: he thus said: "I am the King of Margiana;" he threw Margiana into revolt. One was an impostor named Veisdátes, a Persian: he thus said, "I am Bardes, the son of Cyrus;" he headed a rebellion in Persia. One was an impostor named Aracus, a native of Armenia; he thus said, "I am Nabochodrossor, the son of Nabonidus;" he threw Babylon into revolt.

3 Says Darius the King:—These nine kings I have taken in these battles.

4 Says Darius the King:—These are the provinces

which became rebellious; the God . . . . created lies, that they should deceive the state; afterwards the God Ormazd delivered the state into my hand. As it was desired by me, thus the God Ormazd did.

5 Says Darius the King:—Thou, whoever may be king hereafter, exert thyself to put down lying; the man who may be a liar, him entirely destroy. If thou shalt thus observe my country shall remain entire.

6 Says Darius the King:—This is what I have done. Under the favour of Ormazd, have I always acted. Thou whoever hereafter mayest peruse this tablet let not that which has done by me seem to thee to have been falsely recorded.

7 Says Darius the King:—Ormazd is my witness, (?) that this record (?) I have throughout faithfully executed.

8 Says Darius the King:—By the grace of Ormazd, there is much else that has been done by me that upon this tablet has not been inscribed; on that account it has not been inscribed, lest he who might hereafter peruse this tablet, to him the many deeds (?) that have been done by me else-where, should seem to have been falsely recorded. (?)

9 Says Darius the King:—Those who have been kings before me, by them it has not been done as by me at all times under the favour of Ormazd.

10 Says Darius the King:—Be it known to thee, my successor, that which has been done by me, thus publicly, on that account that thou conceal not. If thou conceal not this edict but publish it to the world, Ormazd shall be a friend to thee, and may thy offspring be numerous, and mayest thou be long lived.

11 Says Darius the King:—If thou shalt conceal this record and not publish it to the world may Ormazd be thy enemy, and mayest thou be childless.

12 Says Darius the King:—This is what I have done;

under the favour of Ormazd, I have always acted. Ormazd has brought help to me, and the other gods which are.

13 Says Darius the King :—On that account Ormazd brought help to me, and the other gods which are, (because) that I was not wicked, nor was I a liar, nor was I a tyrant, neither I nor any of my race. I have obeyed the laws and the rights and customs, I have not violated (?) Whoever laboured for my family, him have I cherished and protected— he who was hostile to me him have I utterly destroyed.

14 Says Darius the King :—Thou who mayest be king hereafter, the man who may be a liar, or who may be an evil doer (?), do not befriend him ; cast him out into utter perdition. (?)

15 Says Darius the King :—Thou whosoever hereafter mayest behold this tablet which I have inscribed, and these figures, beware lest thou injure them ; as long as thou livest, so long shalt thou preserve them.

16 Says Darius the King :—If thou shalt behold this tablet, and these figures, thou shalt not injure ; but shalt preserve them as long as my seed endures, (then) may Ormazd be a friend to thee, and may thy offspring be numerous, and mayest thou be long lived ; and that which thou mayest do may Ormazd bless for thee in aftertimes.

17 Says Darius the King :—If seeing this tablet and these figures, thou shalt injure them, and shalt not preserve them as long as my seed endures, then may Ormazd be thy enemy, and mayest thou be childless ; and that which thou mayest do, may Ormazd curse it for thee.

18 Says Darius the King :—These are the men who alone were there when I slew Gomátes, the Magian, who was called Bardes. These alone, are the men who were my assistants. Intaphernes by name, the son of Veispares a Persian ; Otanes by name, the son of Socris a Persian ; Gobryás by name, the son of Mardonius, a Persian ; Hy-

darnes by name, the son of Megabignes a Persian ; Mega-
byzus by name, the son of Dadoes a Persian ; Ardomanes
by name, the son of Osoces a Persian.

19 Says Darius the King :—Thou who mayest be king
hereafter remember to show favour to the descendants of
these men (?). . . . .

[End of Column IV., which contains ninety-two lines, the
greater part lamentably injured.]

COLUMN V.

Of the thirty-five lines which compose a supplementary half column, divided into 6 Paragraphs, it is impossible to give a complete translation, one side of the tablet being entirely destroyed. From such portions as are decypherable it appears to contain an account of two other revolts ; one in Susiana, conducted by a man named . . . . . . imim ; and the other by Saku'ka, the chief of the Sacæ, who dwelt upon the Tigris.

Darius employed Gubaruwa (Gobryas) the Persian, against the former rebel, and he marched in person against the latter, having previously returned from Media to Babylon. The details of the campaigns cannot be recovered, but they both terminated successfully.

The inscription then concludes with further thanksgivings to Ormazd, and injunctions to the posterity of Darius to preserve uninjured the memorial of his deeds.

The events described in the supplemental column must have taken place during the process of engraving the pre-ceding record, and after the tablet containing the sculptured figures was finished. By a further smoothening of the face of the rock, Darius was enabled to add the Sacan Saku'ka, whom he had defeated in person, to his exhibition of captive figures, but there was no room on the tablet for the figure of the Susian rebel, who was discomfited by his lieutenant Gobryas.

Translation of the detached Inscriptions which are appended to each of the Figures exhibited on the Upper Triumphal Tablet.

Above the head of Darius is an inscription of eighteen lines, containing an exact copy of the four first paragraphs of Column I., which have been already given. The writing is perfect, and the portions, therefore, of the lower tablet which have been effaced, can be determinately restored. It is needless to repeat the translation.

B. Tablet attached to the prostrate figure on which the victor king tramples :—
" This Gomátes, the Magian, was an impostor; he thus declared, ' I am Bardes, the son of Cyrus.   I am the King.'"

C. Adjoining the first standing figure :—
" This Atrines was an impostor ; he thus declared, ' I am King of Susiana.' "

D. Adjoining the second standing figure :—
" This Nadinta-belus was an impostor; he thus declared, ' I am Nabochodrossor, the son of Nabonidus ; I am King of Babylon.' "

E. Adjoining the third standing figure :—'
" This Phraortes was an impostor; he thus declared, ' I am Xathrites, of the race of Cyaxares; I am King of Media.' "

F. Above the fourth standing figure :—
" This Martes was an impostor ; he thus declared, ' I am Imanes, the King of Susiana.' "

G. Adjoining the fifth standing figure :—
" This Sitratachmes was an impostor; he thus declared, ' I am King of Sagartia, of the race of Cyaxares.' "

H. Adjoining the sixth standing figure :—
" This Veisdátes was an impostor; he thus declared, ' I am Bardes, the son of Cyrus.   I am the King.' "

' The Arian legend is engraved on the body of the figure.

I. Adjoining the seventh standing figure :—

"This Aracus was an impostor; he thus declared, ' I am Nabochodrossor, the son of Nabonidus.   I am the King of Babylon.' "

J. Adjoining the eighth standing figure :—

"This Phraates was an impostor; he thus declared, ' I am the King of Margiana.' "

K. Above the ninth or supplemental figure with the high cap :—

"This is Sakuka, the Sacan.' "

BABYLONIAN EXORCISMS.

TRANSLATED BY

REV. A. H. SAYCE, M.A.

THE charms translated below will illustrate the superstition of the Assyrians and Babylonians. Like the Jews of the Talmud they believed that the world was swarming with noxious spirits who produced the various diseases to which man is liable, and might be swallowed with the food and the drink that support life. They counted no less than 300 spirits of heaven and 600 spirits of earth. All this, with the rest of their mythology, was borrowed by the Assyrians from the primitive population of Babylonia, who spoke an agglutinative language akin to the dialects

of the Finnic or Tatar tribes. The charms are
written in this ancient language, but Assyrian translations are appended in a column to the right of the
tablet. The legends are lithographed in the " *Cuneiform Inscriptions of Western Asia,*" vol ii, plates
17 and 18.

TRANSLATION OF THE EXORCISMS.

TABLET I.

May the noxious spirit of the neck, the neck-spirit of the desert, the neck-spirit of the land, the neck-spirit of the sea, the neck-spirit of *the river*, the noxious cherub of the city, the noxious wind, from the man himself (and) the clothing of the body be driven forth ; from the noxious neck-spirit may the king of heaven preserve, may the king of earth preserve.

TABLET II.

From the burning spirit of the entrails which devours the man, from the spirit of the entrails which works evil, may the king of heaven preserve, may the king of earth preserve.

TABLET III.

From wasting, from want of health, from the evil spirit of the ulcer, from spreading quinsey of the gullet, from the violent ulcer, from the noxious ulcer, may the king of heaven preserve, may the king of earth preserve.

TABLET IV.

From sickness of the entrails, from sickness of the heart, from the palpitation of a sick heart, from sickness of bile, from sickness of the head, from noxious colic, from the *agitation* of terror, from flatulency[1] of the entrails, from

---

[1] Literally "opposition."

noxious illness, from lingering sickness, from nightmare, may the king of heaven preserve, may the king of earth preserve.

TABLET V.

From the sweeper-away of buildings, from the robber, from an injured face, from an injured eye, from an injured mouth, from an injured tongue, from injured lips, from an injured *nose*, may the king of heaven preserve, may the king of earth preserve.

TABLET VI.

From the cruel spirit of the head, from the strong spirit of the head, from the head-spirit that departs not, from the head-spirit that goes not forth, from the head-spirit that will not go, from the noxious head-spirit may the king of heaven preserve, may the king of earth preserve.

TABLET VII.

From the poisonous spittle of the mouth[1] which is noxious to the voice, from the phlegm which is destructive to the . . . . . . , from the pustules of the *lungs*, from the pustule of the body, from the loss of the nails, from the removal (and) dissolving of old *excrement*, from the *skin* which is *stripped off*, from the recurrent ague of the body, from the food which hardens in a man's body, from the food which returns after being eaten, from the drink which is *exhaled* after drinking, from death by poison, from the swallowing of the mouth which is *exhaled*, from the unreturning wind from the desert, may the king of heaven preserve, may the king of earth preserve.

[1] That would be consumption.

TABLET VIII.

May Nin-cigal,[1] the wife of Nin-a'su, turn her face to-wards another place ; may the noxious spirit go forth and seize another ; may the female-cherub and the female-demon settle upon his body : may the king of heaven preserve, may the king of earth preserve.

TABLET IX.

May Nebo, the great steward, the recliner (or *incubus*) supreme among the gods, like the god who has begotten him, seize upon his head ; the father of his family may he not injure : may the king of heaven preserve, may the king of earth preserve.

TABLET X.

(On) the sick man by means of sacrifices may perfect health shine like bronze ; may the Sun-god give this man life ; may Merodach, the eldest son of the deep (give him) strength, prosperity, (and) health : may the king of heaven preserve, may the king of earth preserve.

---

[1] Nin-cigal, "The Lady of the Mighty Earth," was Queen of Hades and a form of Allat or Istar. She is also identified with Gula or Bahu (the *Bohu* or "Chaos" of Gen. i. 2), "The Lady of the House of Death," and wife of Hea or Nin-a'su.

WILL OF
SENNACHERIB KING OF ASSYRIA.

TRANSLATED BY

Rev. A. H. SAYCE, M.A.

A TRANSLATION of the private Will of Sennacherib may suitably be connected with the following translated specimens of Assyrian traffic and mercantile customs. It is moreover the earliest example of a Will extant. The original document is printed in the third volume of the *"Cuneiform Inscriptions of Western Asia,"* pl. 16, No. 3.

I, Sennacherib, king of multitudes, king of Assyria, have given chains of gold, stores of ivory, a *cup* of gold, crowns and chains besides, all the riches of which there are heaps, crystal and another precious stone and bird's stone: one and a half manehs, two and a half cibi, according to their weight: to Essar-haddon my son, who was afterwards named Assur-ebil-mucin-pal according to my wish; the treasure of the Temple of Amuk and (Nebo)-irik-erba, the *harpists* of Nebo.

ASSYRIAN

PRIVATE CONTRACT-TABLETS.

TRANSLATED BY

REV. A. H. SAYCE, M.A.

THE following private contract-tablets will give some idea of the activity of trade and business in Western Asia in the 7th and 8th centuries B.C. In consequence of the overthrow of Tyre, Carchemish seems to have become the chief commercial centre of the Eastern world. The clay-tablets are attested by the seal-impressions, or in lieu thereof, by the nail-marks, of the parties to whom they belonged. Several of them have dockets attached, written in the Phœnician character ; and these bilingual legends are valuable corroborations of the accuracy of Assyrian decipherment. The tablets here translated will be found in the "*Cuneiform Inscriptions of Western Asia,*" vol. iii, plates 46-50.

TRANSLATION OF THE TABLETS.

TABLET I.

Ten shekels of the best silver, (being) chains for Istar of Nineveh, which Billu-baladh, in the presence of Manu-ci-Arbela [here follow 3 seals], has lent on a loan; the silver is to have interest paid upon it at 4 per cent. On the 3rd day of the month the silver has been given. (Dated) 3rd day of the month Sebat, during the eponymy of Rimmon-sallim-ani.[1] The witnesses (were): Khattal-munu, Rahu, Kulduin, Neriglissor, Arakh-Nebo the Serippian, Musezib-Assur, Nebo-sallim-sunu, Khanni, (and) Bil-sadan.

[Then follow two lines and a half of Phœnician, the first of which consists of the proper name, Mannugi-Arbela.]

TABLET II.

Two talents of iron, the property of Istar of Arbela, which Mannu-ci-Arbela, in the presence of Samas-akhi-erib, in the month of Ab gives; if they are not given back, at 3 per cent. shall be the interest upon them. On the 11th day of the month Sivan during the eponymy of Bamba;[2] before the witnesses: Istar-bab-esses, Kua, Sarru-ikbi, Dumku-pani-sarri, (and) Nabua.

TABLET III.

Four manehs of silver according to the standard of Carchemish, which Neriglissar, in the presence of Nebo-sum-iddin, son of Nebo-rahim-baladhi, the Keeper of the Crown, from the city of Dur-Sargon, lends out at 5 shekels of silver per month interest. The 26th day of the month Iyyar, during the Eponymy of Gabbaru.[3] The witnesses

[1] In B.C. 650-640.   [2] B.C. 676. .   [3] B.C. 667.

(were) : Nebo-pal-iddin, Nebo-atsib, the holder of the two sceptres, Akhi-ramu, of the same office, Assur-danin-sarri, of the same office, Disi the astronomer, Samas-igur . . , Sin mati-kali the executioner, (and) Merodach . . . . the astronomer.

TABLET IV.

The seal of Ebed-Istar, the master of the men. The giving-up of Hoshea, his two wives Mih'sa (and) Badia, 'Sigaba, Bel-kharran-cunucci, (and) his two daughters, in all 7 persons, slaves, whom Ebed-Istar has sold ; and 'Simadi for 3 manehs of silver has taken. The whole sum hast thou given. The exchange (and) the contract are finished : (there is) no withdrawal. The witnesses (are) Bel-nuri the *priest*, Amyatehu, 'Sangi, Kat-i'sa (and) 'Sidur. [The name of the 6th witness is not filled in]. The month Tisri ; the Eponymy of Dananu.[1]

[Then follow two lines of Phœnician.]

TABLET V.

The nail-mark of Sarru-ludari, the nail-mark of Atar-'suru, (and) the nail-mark of the woman Amat-'Suhala, the wife of Bel-duru, the . . . . . . , the owner of the house (which) is given up. [Then follow 4 nail marks.] The whole house with its woodwork, and its doors, situated in the city of Nineveh, adjoining the houses of Mannu-ci-akhi and] Ilu-ciya, (and) the property of 'Sukaki he has sold, and Tsillu-Assur the astronomer, an Egyptian, for one maneh of silver (according to) the royal (standard), in the presence of Sarru-ludari, Atar-'suru, and Amat-'suhala, the wife of its owner, has received it. The full sum thou hast given. This house has been taken possession of. The exchange (and)

---

[1] Cir. B.C. 680.

the contract are concluded. (There is) no withdrawal.
Whosoever (shall act) feloniously among any of these men
who have sworn to the contract and the agreement, which
(is) before (our) prince Assur, 10 manehs of silver shall he
pay. The witnesses (are): Su'san-kukhadnanis, Murmaza
the . . . . . , Ra'suah the pilot, Nebo-dur-sanin the parti-
tioner of the enemy, Murmaza the pilot, Sinnis-nacarat, (and)
Zedekiah. The 16th day of the month Sivan, the eponymy
of Zazā[1] of the city of Arpad, before Samas-itsbat-nacara,
Latturu, (and) Nebo-sum-yutsur.

[1] B.C. 692.

LEGEND OF ISHTAR

DESCENDING TO HADES.

TRANSLATED BY

H. F. TALBOT, F.R.S., Etc.

THIS very curious Legend is found on a tablet in the British Museum marked K 162.

Some years ago I received a photograph of it, from which I made a translation in 1865, which was published in the *Transactions of the Royal Society of Literature*, vol. 8, p. 244. But about one third of the tablet had been broken off, which materially damaged the sense. Since that time Mr. G. Smith has discovered in the Museum the missing portion of the tablet, and it is now nearly entire. I published another translation (including this new portion) in the *Transactions of the Society of Biblical Archæology*, vol. 2, p. 179 (June 1873) and Mr. Smith has published a translation in the *Daily Telegraph* of August 19, 1873 in which many difficult passages are cleared up. I have carefully revised these translations and think that the general sense of the Legend is now well established.

ISHTAR was the goddess of Love; answering to the Venus of the Latins and the Aphrodite of the Greeks.

The object of her descent into the infernal regions was probably narrated in another tablet, which has not been preserved: for no motive is assigned for it here. I conjecture that she was in search of her beloved Thammuz-Adonis who was detained in Hades by Persephone or Proserpine. We may compare the Greek legend, which was as follows, as given by Panyasis (quoted by Apollodorus)—

"Aphrodite had intrusted Adonis, who was a very beautiful "Child, during his infancy to the care of Persephone; but "she fell in love with him, and refused to restore him. Upon "this Aphrodite appealed to Jupiter, who gave judgment in "the cause. He decreed that Adonis should remain for one "third of the year in the infernal regions with Persephone: "one third of the year in heaven with Aphrodite: the "remaining third of the year was to be at his own disposal. "Adonis chose to spend it in heaven with Aphrodite."[1] The Assyrian legend differs much from this, but yet has some resemblance.

[1] Creuzer's Symbolik vol. 2, p. 423.

COLUMN I.

1 To the land of Hades, the region of (. . . . . .)
2 Ishtar daughter of the Moon-god San turned her mind,
3 and the daughter of San fixed her mind [*to go there*]:
4 to the House of Eternity: the dwelling of the god
Irkalla:
5 to the House men enter—but cannot depart from:
6 to the Road men go—but cannot return.
7 The abode of darkness and famine
8 where Earth is their food: their nourishment Clay:
9 light is not seen: in darkness they dwell:
10 ghosts, like birds, flutter their wings there;
11 on the door and gate-posts the dust lies undisturbed.

12 When Ishtar arrived at the gate of Hades
13 to the keeper of the gate a word she spoke:
14 "O keeper of the entrance! open thy gate!
15 "Open thy gate! again, that I may enter!
16 "If thou openest not thy gate, and I enter not,
17 "I will assault the door: I will break down the gate:
18 "I will attack the entrance: I will split open the
"portals:
19 "I will raise the dead, to be the devourers of the living!
20 "Upon the living, the dead shall prey!"[1]
21 Then the Porter opened his mouth and spoke,
22 and said to the great Ishtar,
23 "Stay, Lady! do not shake down the door!
24 "I will go, and tell this to the Queen Nin-ki-gal."[2]

[1] This very violent language is evidently introduced by the writer of this Legend, in order to justify the subsequent wrath of Proserpine.
[2] Nin-ki-gal answers to the Proserpine of the Latins. Her name means "goddess of the great region," *i. e.* Hades.

25 The Porter entered, and said to Nin-ki-gal,

26 "These curses thy sister Ishtar [*utters*]¹

27 "blaspheming thee with great curses." [. . . . .]

28 When Nin-ki-gal heard this, [. . . .]

29 she grew pale, like a flower that is cut off:

30 she trembled, like the stem of a reed:

31 "I will cure her rage, she said; I will cure her fury:

32 "these curses I will repay to her!

33 "Light up consuming flames! light up blazing straw!

34 "Let her doom be with the husbands who deserted
"their wives!

35 "Let her doom be with the wives who from their hus-
"bands' side departed!

36 "Let her doom be with the youths who led dishonoured
"lives!

37 "Go, Porter, open the gate for her,

38 "but strip her, like others at other times."

39 The Porter went and opened the gate.

40 "Enter, Lady of Tiggaba² city! It is permitted!

41 "May the Sovereign of Hades rejoice at thy presence!"³

42 The first gate admitted her, and stopped her: there
was taken off the great Crown from her head.

43 "Keeper! do not take off from me, the great Crown
"from my head!"

44 "Excuse it, Lady! for the Queen of the land com-
"mands its removal."

-----

45 The second gate admitted her, and stopped her:
there were taken off the earrings of her ears.

¹ The end of this and several following lines is broken off, which makes
the translation uncertain.

² A principal seat of Ishtar's worship.

³ These words are evidently ironical.

46 " Keeper! do not take off from me, the earrings of " my ears!"

47 " Excuse it, Lady! for the Queen of the land com- " mands their removal!"

---

48 The third gate admitted her, and stopped her: there were taken off the precious stones from her head.

49 " Keeper! do not take off from me, the precious stones " from my head!"

50 " Excuse it, Lady! for the Queen of the land com- " mands their removal!"

---

51 The fourth gate admitted her, and stopped her: there were taken off the small lovely gems from her forehead.

52 " Keeper! do not take off from me, the small lovely " gems from my forehead!"

53 " Excuse it, Lady! for the Queen of the land com- " mands their removal!"

---

54 The fifth gate admitted her, and stopped her: there was taken off the central girdle of her waist.

55 " Keeper! do not take off from me, the central girdle " from my waist!"

56 " Excuse it, Lady! for the Queen of the land com- " mands its removal!"

---

57 The sixth gate admitted her, and stopped her: there were taken off the golden rings of her hands and feet.

58 " Keeper! do not take off from me, the golden rings of " my hands and feet!"

11

59 " Excuse it, Lady ! for the Queen of the land com-
" mands their removal ! "

---

60 The seventh gate admitted her, and stopped her :
there was taken off the last garment from her body.

61 " Keeper ! do not take off from me, the last garment
" from my body ! "

62 " Excuse it, Lady ! for the Queen of the land com-
" mands its removal ! "

---

63 After that mother Ishtar had descended into Hades

64 Nin-ki-gal saw her, and stormed on meeting her.

65 Ishtar lost her reason ; and heaped curses upon her.

66 Nin-ki-gal opened her mouth and spoke,

67 to Namtar her messenger a command she gave :

68 " Go, Namtar ! " [*some words lost*]

69 " Bring her out for punishment . . . . " [1]

---

[1] The end of this line is lost, and all the remaining lines of Column I.
are similarly mutilated ; I will therefore give their meaning in an abridged
form. Namtar is commanded to afflict Ishtar with dire diseases of the
eyes, the side, the feet, the heart, and the head. The story then says,
that after the goddess of Love had descended to Hades, the world soon
felt the loss of her influence. But as these lines are much broken, and are
better preserved in the second Column, where they are repeated, I omit
them here.

COLUMN II.

1 The divine messenger of the gods, lacerated his face before them.[1]

2 The assembly of the gods was full,[2]

3 the Sun came, along with the Moon his father.

4 Weeping he spoke thus unto Hea the king:

5 "Ishtar descended into the earth; and she did not "rise again:

6 "and since the time that mother Ishtar descended "into Hades,

7 "the bull has not sought the cow, nor the male of "any animal the female.

8 "The slave and her master [*some words lost*]

9 "The master has ceased from commanding:

10 "the slave has ceased from obeying."

11 Then the god Hea in the depth of his mind laid a plan:

12 he formed, for her escape, the figure of a man of clay.[3]

13 "Go to save her, Phantom! present thyself at the "portal of Hades;

14 "the seven gates of Hades will open before thee,

15 "Nin-ki-gal will see thee, and be pleased with thee.

16 "When her mind shall be grown calm, and her anger "shall be worn off,

17 "awe her with the names of the great gods!

[1] A sign of violent grief in the East. Forbidden in Deut. xiv. 1; Lev. xix. 28. The bleeding face betokened a Messenger of Evil News.

[2] Line injured: sense doubtful.

[3] The original has *Assinnu*, which I have derived from the Chaldee word *Sin* "clay." But this is a mere conjecture. The meaning evidently is, that Hea moulded a figure and breathed life into it. Hea was the god to whom all clever inventions were attributed. "*Lord of deep thoughts*" was one of his most usual titles.

18 "Prepare thy frauds! On deceitful tricks fix thy "mind!

19 "The chiefest deceitful trick! Bring forth fishes of the "waters out of an empty vessel!¹

20 "This thing will please Nin-ki-gal:

21 "then to Ishtar she will restore her clothing.

22 "A great reward for these things shall not fail.

23 "Go, save her, Phantom! and the great assembly of "the people shall crown thee!

24 "Meats, the first of the city, shall be thy food!

25 "Wine, the most delicious in the city, shall be thy drink!

26 "To be the Ruler of a Palace, shall be thy rank!

27 "A throne of state, shall be thy seat!

28 "Magician and Conjuror shall bow down before thee!"

---

29 Nin-ki-gal² opened her mouth and spoke:

30 to Namtar her messenger a command she gave:

31 "Go, Namtar! clothe the Temple of Justice!³

32 "Adorn the *images?* and the *altars?*

33 "Bring out Anunnak!⁴ Seat him on a golden throne!

34 "Pour out for Ishtar the waters of life, and let her "depart from my dominions!"

35 Namtar went; and clothed the Temple of Justice;

36 he adorned the images and the altars;

---

¹ The present legend was probably a kind of Miracle Play which was actually performed in one of the temples. Juggling tricks, which have been known in the East from time immemorial (vide Pharaoh's magicians) were probably introduced for the amusement of the audience. Only one is related here, but there may have been many more.

² The things commanded are now supposed to have been successfully performed.

³ This seems to be the final scene of the Play, representing a magnificent hall or palace.

⁴ A Genius, who is often mentioned. Here he seems to act the part of a judge, pronouncing the absolution of Ishtar.

37 he brought out Anunnak ; on a golden throne he seated him ;

38 he poured out for Ishtar the waters of life, and let her go.

39 Then the first gate let her forth, and restored to her— the first garment of her body.

40 The second gate let her forth, and restored to her— the diamonds of her hands and feet.

41 The third gate let her forth, and restored to her— the central girdle of her waist.

42 The fourth gate let her forth, and restored to her— the small lovely gems of her forehead.

43 The fifth gate let her forth, and restored to her—the precious stones of her head.

44 The sixth gate let her forth, and restored to her—the earrings of her ears.

45 The seventh gate let her forth, and restored to her— the great Crown on her head. '

' Her ornaments are restored to her exactly in the reverse order that they were taken off.

NOTE. There are 13 more lines, but they are much broken, and they appear not to relate to the above Legend. At any rate they belong to another Chapter of it which has not been hitherto alluded to. A satisfactory translation of them can therefore hardly be given.

ASSYRIAN

ASTRONOMICAL TABLETS.

SELECTED AND TRANSLATED BY

REV. A. H. SAYCE, M.A.

THE following are specimens of the numerous astronomical and astrological reports with which the Libraries of Assyria and Babylonia abounded. The tablets from which the translations are made come from the Library of Assurbanipal: but the larger part of them are merely later editions of works composed for Babylonian kings before the 16th century B.C. This is the date of the great astrological work, consisting of 72 tablets or volumes, a small portion of which is translated below. The inscription numbered VII. has already been translated by Dr. Oppert. The originals will be found in the "*Cuneiform Inscriptions of Western Asia,*" vol. iii, plates 51, 54, 58, 59, 60, 61. It is much to be regretted that many of the records are in a very fragmentary condition, the first and final lines of the terra cotta being lost.

TRANSLATION OF THE TABLETS.

TABLET I.

1 (On) the 6th day of Nisan (March)
2 the day and the night
3 were balanced (*i.e.* were equal).
4 (There were) 6 hours of day
5 and 6 hours of night.
6 May Nebo (and) Merodach
7 to the king my lord
8 be propitious.

TABLET II.

1 (On) the 15th day of Nisan
2 the day and the night
3 were balanced.
4 (There were) 6 hours of day
5 and 6 hours of night.
6 May Nebo (and) Merodach
7 to the king my lord
8 be propitious.

TABLET III.

1 A watch we kept.
2 (On) the 29th day the moon
3 we saw.
4 May Nebo (and) Merodach
5 to the king my lord
6 be propitious.
7 (The report) of Nabu
8 of the city of Assur[1]

[1] Kileh-Shergat.

TABLET IV.

1 To the king my lord
2 thy servant Istar-iddina
3 Chief (Astronomer),
4 of the city of Arbela.
5 May there be peace
6 to the king my lord.
7 May Nebo (and) Merodach
8 (and) Istar of Arbela
9 to the king my lord
10 be propitious.
11 On the 29th day
12 a watch
13 we kept.   The moon we did not see.
14 In the month Tammuz (June), the 2nd day,
15 during the eponymy of Bel-sunu
16 Prefect of the city of Khindana.

TABLET V.

1 (If) the moon the 1st day is seen,
2 the face is stedfast,
3 the heart of the country is good.
4 (If) the moon at its appearance has a halo,
5 the king to supremacy
6 goes.
7 (Report of) Nergal-edir.

TABLET VI.

1 To the king, my lord,
2 thy servant Istar-iddina
3 the Chief
4 of the Astronomers,
5 of the city of Arbela.

6 May there be peace
7 to the king my lord.
8 May Nebo, Merodach
9 (and) Istar of Arbela
10 to the king my lord
11 be propitious.
12 On the 29th day
13 a watch
14 we kept.
15 (In) the observatory[1]
16 (There was) mist.
17 The moon we did not see.
18 (Dated) the month Sebat,[2] the 1st day
19 during the eponymy of Bel-kharran-sadua.[3]

TABLET VII.

1 To the king my lord, thy servant
2 Abil-Istar.   Peace
3 to the king my lord.   May Nebo (and) Merodach
4 to the king my lord be propitious.
5 Long days, soundness of flesh
6 and joy of heart may the great gods
7 to the king my lord grant.   (On) the 27th day
8 the moon is fixed.   (On) the 28th day,
9 the 29th day (and) the 30th day a watch
10 for an eclipse of the Sun we kept.
11 The sun behind the shadow (of the eclipse) did not
pass.
12 (On) the 1st day the moon was seen in the day
time,

[1] Literally "House of Observation."   [2] Our January.

[3] The report accordingly was sent in to Assurbanipal, as Bel-kharran-sadua was eponym during his reign.   The year, according to Mr. Smith would be 649 B.C.

13 during the month Tammuz current,

14 above the planet Mercury ;

15 of which I have already

16 to the king my lord sent this[1]

17 account.   During the period of 5 days when the moon is called Anu[2]

18 in the circle of the star Shepherd of the Heavenly Flock

19 it was seen declining.[3]

20 By reason of rain the horns were not visible

21 *very clearly*.   Thus

22 during this 5 days' period when the moon is Anu

23 in regard to its conjunction to the king my lord

24 I have sent.   Thus

25 it extended itself (and) was visible

26 below the star of the Chariot.

27 During the 5 days' period when the moon's course is called Bel[4] it is fixed ;

28 round the star of the Chariot it turned its course.

29 Its conjunction was prevented ; but

30 nevertheless its conjunction with Mercury

31 which (took place) during the 5 days' period when the moon is Anu

32 of which I have already to the king my lord

33 sent a special (report)

34 was not prevented.

35 May the king my lord have peace.

---

[1] *I.e.* a special.   [2] *I.e.* from the 1st to the 5th day.

[3] Literally "in the lower part (of the sky)."

[4] The orbit of the moon was called Bel from the 10th to the 15th day, though the heavenly body itself was called Hea, the name it bore also from the 6th to the 10th day. It was termed Anu from the 1st to the 5th day.

TABLET VIII.

1 The 15th day the Moon and the Sun
2 with one another are seen.
3 The face is stedfast. The heart of land is good.
4 Joy possesses the heart of the inhabitants.
5 The gods of Accad
6 to prosperity consign (it).
7 The Moon and the Sun are clear ;
8 the king of the land his ears enlarges.
9 (The report) of Ablua.

TABLET IX.

1 The 15th day, the moon and the sun with (one
another)
2 are seen. A strong enemy
3 his arrows against the land lifts up.
4 The great gate of the city the enemy undermines.
5 The stars in the centre of heaven are obscured by
rain ;
6 the enemy the streams of water makes bitter.

TABLET X.

1 The moon has a dark setting.
2 The month rain continuously and fog
3 will mark.

TABLET XI.

1 The moon sank to rest. The planet Mars
2 in the place of its (setting) was fixed. Destruction of
cattle.
3 The land of Phœnicia is made small.

TABLET XII.[1]

(*Portion of an Astronomical Calendar.*)

15 In the month Sivan (on) the 14th day an eclipse happens ; and in the east it begins and in the west it ends.

16 In the night-watch it begins, and in the morning-watch[2] it ends. Eastward at the time of appearance and cessation

17 its shadow is seen ; and to the king of Dilmun[3] the crown is given. The king of Dilmun on the throne grows old.

18 (On) the 15th day an eclipse takes place. The king of Dilmun on the throne is slain ; and a nobody seizes on the [throne].

19 (On) the 16th day an eclipse happens. The king is slain by his eunuchs, and a plebeian seizes on the (throne.)

20 (On) the 20th day an eclipse takes place. Rains in heaven, floods in the channels flow.

21 (On) the 21st day an eclipse takes place. Devastation or rapine

22 in the country comes about. Corpses in the country are.   (⁴) _____

23 In the month Tammuz (on) the 14th day an eclipse happens ; and in the west it begins and in the south and north it ends.

24 In the evening-watch it begins and in the night-watch it ends. Westward at the time of appearance (and) disappearance

[1] The commencement of this Tablet is lost; the characters left become intelligible at line 15.

[2] The night was divided into three watches, the evening-watch, the night-watch, and the morning-watch. These occupied the 6 *kaspu* or periods of 2 hours assigned to the night. See the Observatory reports numbered I. and II.

[3] Dilmun was a country on the shores of the Persian Gulf.

[4] These lines are in the original, they divide the tablet into months.

25 its shadow is seen ; and to the king of Gutium a crown is given.

26 The forces of Gutium are in service ; submission of (foreign) troops.

27 (On) the 15th day an eclipse takes place. Rains in heaven, floods on the land descend. Famine is in the land.

28 (On) the 16th day an eclipse takes place. Women their offspring do not perfect.

29 (On) the 20th day an eclipse happens. In the month Ab (July) the Air-god his mouth sets : and the god eats.

30 For a year the Air-god the cattle inundates.

31 (On) the 21st day an eclipse takes place. From the king twice his lands revolt, and to the hand of his foes deliver him.

---

32 In the month Ab, the 14th day, an eclipse happens ; and in the south it begins, and in the west it ends.

33 In the evening-watch and in the morning-watch it begins ; and at sun-rise it ends.

34 Southward at the time of appearance (and) disappearance its shadow is seen ; and to the king of Mullias a crown is given.

35 The life of the soldier . . . and the soldiers for a year in a campaign serve, and men by arrows are slain.

36 (On) the 15th day an eclipse takes place. The king dies ; and rains in heaven, floods in the channels are.

37 (On) the 16th day an eclipse takes place. The king of Accad dies. The war-god on the land feeds.

38 (On) the 20th day an eclipse takes place. The king of the Hittites lives and on the throne seizes.

39 (On) the 21st day an eclipse takes place. The god *plagues* the king and the flames devour land and king.

---

40 In the month of Elul (August), the 14th day, an

eclipse takes place; and in the north it begins and in the south

41 and the east it ends. In the evening-watch it begins, and in the night-watch it ends.

42 Northward at the time of appearance (and) disappearance its shadow is seen; and to the king of Mullias a crown is given.

43 To the king the crown is an omen; and over the king the eclipse passes. Rains in heaven,

44 floods in the channels flow. A famine is in the country. Men their sons for silver sell.

45 (On) the 15th day an eclipse takes place. The son of the king murders his father, and on the throne seizes; and the enemy plunders and devours the land.

46 (On) the 16th day an eclipse happens. The king of a foreign country[1] plunders and on the throne seizes.

47 Rain in heaven, a flood in the channels descends.

48 (On) the 20th day an eclipse takes place. Rains in heaven, floods in the channels descend. Country with country keeps festival and makes peace.

49 (On) the 21st day an eclipse takes place. The throne of the foe lasts not. A king self-appointed in the land shall be.

50 After a year the Air-god inundates. Ditto (*i.e.* after a year) the king does not remain. His country is made small.

---

51 In the month Tisri (September), the 14th day, an eclipse happens; and in the south it begins and in the west it ends.

52 In the evening-watch it begins, and in the night-watch it ends. Southward at the time of appearance (and) disappearance

[1] Or the king of the Hittites.

53 its shadow is seen; and to the king of Elam a crown is given. The forces of Elam

54 in service are. *No return* of peace to his men.

55 (On) the 15th day an eclipse takes place. The foe plunders and the corn of the land devours and seizes and over the country tyrannises.

56 (On) the 16th day an eclipse happens. Suddenly the king dies. (There is) division of his kingdom.

57 (On) the 20th day an eclipse takes place. The flame the land consumes. Pregnant women their offspring do not perfect.

58 (On) the 21st day an eclipse takes place. A flight of many birds to a country or to countries happens.

TABLET XIII.[1]

(*Portion of another Calendar.*)

11 Contrary to their calculated time the Moon and the Sun with one another are seen. A strong enemy the country spoils.

12 The king of Accad under his enemy is placed. The 12th day with the Sun (the Moon) is seen˙; and

13 the 12th day the Moon and the Sun with one another are seen. Then terribly the heads of men the executioner cuts off.

14 The 13th day, the same (*i.e.* the Moon and the Sun are seen together). The face (is) not stedfast. The king of the land (is) not prosperous. Under the enemy he is. The enemy in the land campaigns.

15 The 14th day, the same. The face (is) stedfast; the heart of the land is good. The gods consign Accad to prosperity.

[1] The commencement of this Tablet is lost.

16 Joy in the heart of men results. The cattle of Accad in safety in the desert lie down.

17 The 15th day, the same. A powerful enemy his servants to the country sends ; and the great gate of the city the enemy undermines.

18 The 16th day, the same. King to king hostility sends. The king in his palace for the period of a month [remains].

19 The hostile foot against his land is set. The enemy through his country tyrannically marches.

20 The 17th day, the same. The haughty foot (goes) against the land. A foreign tongue over the land is lord.

21 The 20th day the same. The hostile soldier marches and the land rules. The altars of the great gods are taken away.

22 Bel to Elam goes. At last after 30 years the smitten are restored. The great gods with them return.

[1]
___

23 (In) the months of Chisleu,[2] Tebet,[3] (and) Sebat[4] the horn of the moon is double, and in (holy) places (there is) rest from sacrifices.

24 For these three months (on) the 15th day, the sky is not seen; on the 30th day no mists.

25 The Moon its path directs and the Sun during the day goes. The same (*i.e.* the moon directs its path). It is changed from the 15th day of the month Marchesvan[5] to the 15th day of the month Chisleu.[2]

26 The night according to its reckoning is long. The north wind blows. The days of the king of Accad (are) long, the heart of his people (is) good.

27 The same. The night according to its reckoning is long. The north-wind blows. The king of Accad, his days (are) long, his life is extended.

[1] See note 4 page 20.   [2] November.   [3] December.
[4] January.   [5] October.

28 The moon its path directs and the sun during the day goes. The same. It is changed. From the 15th day of the month Tebet to the 15th day of the month Sebat

29 the night according to its stated time is long. The west wind blows. The king of Phœnicia (enjoys) long days. The heart of the people (is) good.

30 The same. The night according to its stated hours (is) long. The west wind blows. The days of the king of Phœnicia (are) long. His life is extended.

---

31 A bright light at the rising of the Sun arises, and in the assembly of the people diffuses itself . . . .

32 The days of the prince (are long).

33 The Sun is ascendant, and a Star after it appears. Peace to (men).

34 (Attack ?) of pestilence violently and the men (die ?)

35 The Sun is in the ascendant and clouds are present
. . . .

36 (In) the month Chisleu, the 20th day (the moon) makes its appearance, and in brilliance the moon (shines).

NOTE :—It may interest our readers to know that the bulk of these Tablets are in the British Museum and are readily accessible to students.

THE ASSYRIAN CALENDAR.

THE Babylonian Year was divided into 12 months of 30 days each, with an intercalary month every 6 years. The night had originally been divided into 3 watches, but afterwards the more accurate division into hours came into use, the day and the night severally containing 6 *casbu* (or *asli* as the Assyrians called them). According to the lunar division, the 7th, 14th, 19th, 21st, and 28th, were days of "rest," on which certain works were forbidden; and the two lunations were divided each into three periods of 5

	ASSYRIAN NAME.	JEWISH (Aramaic) NAME.	ENGLISH MONTH (roughly).
1.	Ni'sannu	Ni'san	March
2.	Airu	Iyyar	April
3.	'Sivanu *or* Tsivan	Sivan	May
4.	Duzu	Tammuz	June
5.	Abu.	Ab	July
6.	Ululu	Elul	August
7.	Tasritu	Tisri	September
8.	Arakh-samna ("the 8th month.")	Marchesvan	October
9.	Cisilivu *or* Cuzallu	Chisleu	November
10.	Dhabitu	Tebet	December
11.	Sabahu	Sebat	January
12.	Addaru	Adar	February
	Arakhu-makru ("the incidental month.")	Ve-Adar	*

days, the 19th ending the first period of the 2nd lunation. Each month was under the protection of some deity, and its Accadian name answers to the corresponding sign of the Zodiac. The Assyrians seem to have once possessed a calendar of their own, in which the months had native names, like the old Jewish Calendar with its Bul, Ethanim, etc. Thus the 3rd month was called "The Royal," and another month *mukhur ili*, "The Gift of the Gods." But along with the Jews they afterwards adopted the Aramaic Calendar, which was based upon that of the Accadians; indeed, the names of the months in this Calendar, wherever they are explicable, seem to be derived from the Accadian titles of the months and Zodiacal signs. This Aramaic-Accadian Calendar began with Nisan.

ACCADIAN NAME.	ZODIACAL SIGN.	DEITY TO WHOM THE MONTH WAS DEDICATED.
Sara zig-gar ("the sacrifice of righteousness.")	Aries (the most usual object of sacrifice.)	Anu and Bel
Khar sidi ("the propitious bull.")	Taurus	Hea
Mun-ga ("of bricks,") & *Kas* ("the twins.")	Gemini	Sin (the moon-god.)
Su kul-na ("seizer of seed.")	Cancer	Adar
Ab ab-gar ("fire that makes fire.")	Leo	"The Queen of the bow."
Ki Gingir-na ("the errand of Istar.")	Virgo	Istar
Tul cu ("the holy altar.")	Libra	Samas (the sun-god.)
Apin am-a ("the bull-liker founder"?)	Scorpio	Merodach
Gan ganna ("the very cloudy.")	Sagittarius	Nergal
Ab-ba uddu ("the father of light."?)	Capricornus	Papsucal
As a-an ("abundance of rain.")	Aquarius	Rimmon (the air-god.)
Se ki-sil ("sowing of seed.")	Pisces	"The 7 Great Gods"
Se dir "dark [month] of sowing.")	*	Assur

ASSYRIAN WEIGHTS AND MEASURES.

COMPILED BY

REV. A. H. SAYCE, M.A.

MEASURES OF LENGTH :—

60 ubani = 1 suklu, rabtu or ammat ("cubit"=20 inches)

6 ammat= 1 kanu ("cane"=10 ft.)

12 kani = 1 ribu or gar

60 ribi = 1 soss

30 sosses = 1 kasbu or aslu ("a day's journey," about 14 miles)
For field measures the square of 60 yards was the unit, and the *soss* was called *ammat-gagar*, containing 360 yards. Sixty of these made one *masku* of 21,600 yards.

WEIGHTS AND MONEYS:—

8 ig or "royal shekels"	=	1 shekel (12 dts.)
60 shekels	=	1 mana-gina (1 lb., 4 oz., 8 dts.
2 mana-gina("standard manehs")	=	1 maneh (2 lbs., 8 oz., 16 dts.)
30 manehs	=	1 talent (82 lbs.)

The talent was according to the standard either of Assyria ("the royal talent" or "the talent of the country") or of Carchemish. The contract-tablets variously give 1 talent of silver as equivalent to 5 manehs of gold, 5 manehs of silver to 2 manehs of gold, 10 manehs of silver to 1 maneh of gold, etc.

MEASURES OF CAPACITY :—

Land and grain were alike measured by the *log* (*lagitu*) which contained respectively 10, 9, and 8 subdivisions called *baru, aru,* and *arrat.* Grain was also measured by the *makaru;* and we find 100 *makarrat* of barley in a contract-tablet. The *arrat* was divided into the "*baru*" or "half of wood" and the "baru of stone."

The tonnage of ships was reckoned by the *gurru;* thus we have ships of 15 and 60 *gurri.*

ASSYRIAN.

ARRANGED BY

GEORGE SMITH.

Works on History and Chronology.

Eponym Canon (Cun. Ins., Vol. III, p. 1).

Historical Canon (Cun. Ins., Vol. II, p. 52).

Synchronous History (Cun. Ins., Vol. II, p. 65).

Historical.

Legends of Izdubar (texts unpublished). (Deluge Tablets.)

Inscriptions of Urukh king of Babylonia (Cun. Ins., Vol. I, p. 1).

Inscriptions of Dungi son of Urukh (Cun. Ins., Vol. I, p. 2).

Inscriptions of various other early Babylonian Sovereigns (Trans. Soc. Bib. Ar., Vol. I, pp. 37 to 46).

Inscription of Sargon I king of Babylonia (Cun. Ins., Vol. III, p. 4).

Inscription of Sargon and his son Naram-sin (Trans. Soc. Bib. Ar., pp. 49-51).

Various Inscriptions of Kudur-mabuk and Rim-sin his son (see Trans. Soc. Bib. Ar., p. 42, and notes).

Early Babylonian Dated Tablets (texts unpublished).

Brick of Samsi-vul I ruler of Assyria (Cun. Ins., Vol. I. p. 6).

Brick of Kara-indas king of Babylon (Trans. Soc. Bib. Ar., p. 68).

Inscriptions of Burna-buriyas king of Babylon (Cun. Ins.,
Vol. I, p. 4, etc.).

Inscriptions of Kuri-galzu king of Babylon (Cun. Ins.,
Vol. I, p. 4, etc.).

Inscriptions of Pudil king of Assyria (Revue Ar., Nov., 1869).

Monolith of Maruduk-bal-idina I king of Babylonia (text
unpublished).

Tablet of Vul-nirari I king of Assyria (text unpublished).

Small Inscriptions of Vul-nirari (various).

Inscriptions of Shalmaneser I king of Assyria (various).

Inscriptions of Tugulti-ninip king of Assyria (various unpublished ; one Cun. Ins., Vol. III, p. 4).

Inscriptions of Assur-risilim king of Assyria (Cun. Ins.,
Vol. III, p. 3).

Brick and Cone Inscriptions of Vul-bal-idina king of Babylon
(various).

Inscriptions of Nebuchadnezzar I king of Babylonia (unpublished).

Cylinder of Tiglath-Pileser I king of Assyria (Cun. Ins.,
Vol. I, pp. 9-16).

Other fragments of Tiglath-Pileser (various).

Contracts dated in the reign of Maruduk-nadin-ahi king of
Babylon (various).

Inscriptions of Assur-bel-kala king of Assyria (Cun. Ins.,
Vol. I, p. 6).

Inscriptions of Samsivul IV king of Assyria (Cun. Ins.,
Vol. III, p. 3).

Contract dated in the reign of Simmas-sihu king of Babylon
(Layard's Ins., p. 53).

Annals of Assur-nazir-pal king of Assyria, from pavement
slabs (Cun. Ins., Vol. I, pp. 17-26).

Other Inscriptions of Assur-nazir-pal (various).

Kurkh Monolith of Shalmaneser II (Cun. Ins., Vol. III,
pp. 7 and 8).

Bull Inscriptions of Shalmaneser II (Layard's Ins., p. 12, etc.).

Black Obelisk of Shalmaneser II (Layard's Ins., p. 87).

Inscriptions of Vul-nirari III king of Assyria (Cun. Ins., Vol. I. p. 35).

Fragments of Annals of Tiglath-Pileser II king of Assyria (various).

Fragments of Inscriptions Shalmaneser IV king of Assyria (various).

Inscription of the Second Year of Sargon (unpublished).

Nimrud Inscription of Sargon (Layard's Ins., p. 33).

Cylinder (Barrel) of Sargon (Cun. Ins., Vol. I, p. 36).

Prism of Sargon (unpublished).

Fastes of Sargon (Botta).

Annals of Sargon (Botta).

Other Inscriptions of Sargon (various).

Tablet of Kalah Shergat.

Nebbi Yunas Tablet (Cun. Ins., Vol. I, pp. 43,44).

Bull Inscriptions of Sennacherib (Cun. Ins., Vol. III, pp. 12 and 13).

Other Inscriptions of Sennacherib (various).

Cylinder of Esarhaddon king of Assyria (Cun. Ins., Vol. I, pp. 45-47).

Various other Inscriptions of Esarhaddon (Cun. Ins. Vol. I, etc.).

Portions of Cylinders B, C, D, and E of Assurbanipal (Smith's Assurbanipal).

Various Historical Tablets of Assurbanipal (Smith's Assurbanipal).

Hunting Texts of Assurbanipal (Cun. Ins., Vol. I, p. 7).

Inscriptions of Assur-ebil-ili king of Assyria (Cun. Ins. Vols. I and III).

Cylinder of Bel-zakir-iskun king of Assyria (Cun. Ins. Vol. I p. 8).

Inscription of Nabopalassar king of Babylonia (unpublished).

Inscription (India House) of Nebuchadnezzar (Cun. Ins.
Vol. I, pp. 53 to 64).

Senkereh Cylinder of Nebuchadnezzar (Cun. Ins., Vol. I,
p. 51).

Borsippa Cylinder of Nebuchadnezzar (Cun. Ins., Vol. I,
p. 51).

Various other Texts of Nebuchadnezzar.

Tablet dated in the reign of Evil Merodach king of Babylon.

Cylinder of Nergal-shar-ezer king of Babylon (Cun. Ins.,
Vol. I, p. 67).

Cylinders of Nabonidas king of Babylon (Cun. Ins., Vol. I,
pp. 68, 69).

Other texts of Nabonidas (various).

Brick of Cyrus king of Babylon, (Trans. Soc. Bib. Ar., Vol. II,
pt. I).

Inscription on Tomb of Cyrus.

Dated Tablets in reign of Cambyses (various).

Inscriptions of Darius.

Inscriptions of Xerxes king of Persia.

Inscriptions of Artaxerxes king of Persia.

Later Inscriptions of Persian, Greek, and Parthian periods.

Mythology and Religion (mostly unpublished).

History of the Evil Spirits.

Hymn to the Moon God.

Hymns to Ninip.

The War of the Gods.

Incantations for removing Curses.

Prayers of Amil-urgal.

Prayer against Eclipses.

Various other Prayers.

Various Mythological Stories and Invocations.

Tablets against Witchcraft.

Fable (unpublished).

The Horse and the Ox.

Government (mostly unpublished).

Tablet with Advice and Cautions to Kings.
Various Reports and Despatches.
Various Tablets with Laws and Law Cases.

Private Life.

Further Deeds of Sale and Barter.
Further Loan Tablets.
Private Letters.
Lists of Property.

Science, etc. (partly unpublished).

Geographical Lists.
Lists of Animals and Birds.
Lists of Minerals and their uses.
Lists of Wooden Objects.
Grammatical Tablets (a selection from).
Mathematical Tablets.

Astrology and Astronomy.

Further Selections from the great Chaldean Work on Astrology.
Further Selections from Astronomical and Astrological Reports.
A Selection of Omens from Terrestrial Objects and Events.[1]

PHŒNICIAN.

Sarcophagus of Ashmunazer (Duc de Luynes, *Mémoire,* 1856).
Marseilles Inscription (Judas, 1857).
The Moabite Stone (Ginsburg, 1871).
Selected Mortuary Inscriptions.

[1] Selections of these only printed in Vol. I.

EGYPTIAN.

(*Tentative List only.*)

P. LE PAGE RENOUF, F.R.S.L.

Historical Documents.

Ancient Empire :

    Inscription of Unas (Rougé, Six premières dynasties).

        ,,   Tomb of Ameni (Benihassan I).

        ,,   Tomb of Nahre-si Chnum-hotep (Beni-hassan II).

XVIIIth Dynasty :

    Inscription of Aahmes son of Abna (Denk. III, pl. 12).

        ,,   Aahmes, formerly called Pensouvan (Louvre C, 49).

        ,,   Thotmes I at Karnak (Denk. III, 18).

        ,,   Hatasu (Duemichen, Hist. Ins., 19, 20).

    Annals of Thothmes III (Birch, Rougé, Brugsch).

    Other Monuments of Thothmes III (Birch and De Rougé Rougé).

    Inscription of Amem-em-heb at Abd-el-Gurnah (Ebers).

    Inscriptions of Amenophis III (Denk. III, 65 and following).

    Monuments of the Disk Worshippers.

XIXth Dynasty :

    Triumphal Inscription of Seti I at Karnak (Denk. III, 126).

Inscription of Seti I at Radesieh.

The Great Harris Papyrus of Rameses II.

Dedicatory Inscription of Rameses II at Abydos (Maspéro).

Treaty of Rameses II with King of the Cheta (Denk. III, 146).

Great Triumphal Inscription of Rameses II, (Denk. III, 153).

Triumphal Inscriptions (Denk. III, 165, etc).

Historical Inscription at Abusimbel (187).

Great Tablet at Abusimbel (194).

Tablet of the Year 400 (Révue Arch).

Inscription of Bek-en-Chonsu (Déveria).

Journey in Syria, etc. (1st Anastasi Papyrus, Chabas and Goodwin).

XXth Dynasty :

Inscription of Seti II (Duemichen, Hist. Ins., 1 to 5).

,, Rameses III (Rosellini, Burton, Greene, and Duemichen, *ubi supra* 13 to 15).

XXIst Dynasty :

Tablet 4th year of Rameses IV.

Tablet of Temple of Chronos at Karnak.

Ethiopic period :

Pianchi Inscription.

Dream Tablet.

"Stèle de l'inthronisation." ⎫
 ⎬ Mariette's Monuments.
"Stèle de l'excommunication." ⎭

Persian and Ptolemaic :

Statuette Naophore du Vatican.

Tablet of Tafnecht at Naples.

Inscription of Ptolemy son of Lagos.

Tablet of Canopus.
   „   Rosetta.
"Bauurkunde der Templelanlagen von Edfu" (Due-
   michen).
Two Ptolemaic Tablets (Birch).
Selection of Obelisk Inscriptions.
   „   Apis Tablets.

Religious or Magical Texts.

Ancient Forms of Sepulchral Offerings, etc.   (Tablets of
   Ancient Empire).
Book of the Dead.
Spells in Lepsius ("Aelteste Texte").
Harris Magical Papyrus.
Magical Text in British Museum (Salt 825.   Birch).
"Horus on Crocodiles" (various texts, Leyden and elsewhere).
Spells in Tomb of Bek-en-ren-ef.
" Metternich Tablet."
" *Shâ en sensenu ;*" the "Book of the Breaths of Life."
Lamentations of Isis (Horrack).
Legend of Horus (Naville).
Rhind Papyri.
Sarcophagus of Seti (Bonomi).
   „   Necht-en-heb.
   „   T'at-hra (Louvre).
   „   British Museum, 32.
Litanies of the Sun (Denk. III, 203).
Selection of Hymns, such as the following :
   Ap-heru-mes (Berlin, in Brugsch Monumens, pl. III).
   Meri   („   „   „   pl. IV).
   To Osiris (Bibliothèque Nationale, Chabas).
   Fragments of the Hymns of the Disk Worshippers.
   Several in British Museum.
      „   Duemichen's publications.

Great Psalm to Ammon (Leyden I, 350).

Calendar of Lucky and Unlucky Days (Sallier, Chabas).

Calendars of Festivals from as Early Date as possible to Roman Period.

Literature, Philosophy, Science, Economy.

Proverbs, Prisse Papyrus.

Tale of " Saneha " (Goodwin).

,,   " Two Brothers."

,,   Setnau (Brugsch, Rev. Arch).

" Rules of Life" (Papyrus at Bulaq, lately published by Marriette).

Song of the Oxen (Denk. III, 10).

Poem of Pentaur.

Medical Papyrus (Berlin).

,,   ,,   (British Museum).

Geometrical Papyrus (British Museum).

Letters on all varieties of subjects in the Sallier, Anastasi, and Leyden Papyri.

Registers, etc., (Rollin and other Papyri).

Accounts.

Receipts for making Kyphi, etc.

Catalogues of the Temple Library at Edfu.

Law and Police.

Abbott Papyrus (Spoliation of Tombs).

" Pap. Judiciare de Turin " (Devéria).

Report on Capture of Fugitive Slaves (Leyden I, 368, Chabas).

Complaint against Paneba (British Museum, Salt, Chabas).

Petition to king Amenophis (Chabas).

Complaint against Thefts committed by certain Workmen (Chabas).

Will be ready in July, 1874.

RECORDS OF THE PAST.
VOL. II.
EGYPTIAN TEXTS,
Containing among others the following Translations :—

Annals of Thothmes III.
> By Dr. BIRCH, F.S.A.

Hymns to Amun (*Anastasi Papyri*).
> By C. W. GOODWIN, M.A.

Voyage of an Egyptian to Syriæ.
> By M. FRANÇOIS CHABAS.

Lamentations of Isis for Osiris.
> By M. de HORRACK.

The Tale of the Two Brothers (*D'Orbigny Papyrus*).
> By M. MASPERO.

The Wars of Rameses II. against the Hittites (*Sallier Papyrus*).
> By Prof. LUSHINGTON, M.A.

The Story of Saneha.
> By C. W. GOODWIN, M.A.

The Inscription of Pianchi Mer-amon (*Pianchi Stèle*).
> By Canon COOK, M.A.

Stèle of Ahmès and Newer-hotep (*Louvre Coll.*)
> By M. PIERRET.

SAMUEL BAGSTER AND SONS,
15, PATERNOSTER ROW.

Printed in the United States
88579LV00007B/231/A